Pe
in
Midd

David Astor and Valerie Yorke

Peace
in the
Middle East

Foreword by Lord Harlech

CORGI
A Division of Transworld Publishers Ltd

PEACE IN THE MIDDLE EAST
A CORGI BOOK 0 552 98077 3

First Publication in Great Britain

PRINTING HISTORY
Corgi edition published 1978 by arrangement with Transworld
Publishers and The World Security Trust.

Corgi Books are published by Transworld Publishers Ltd,
Century House, 61–63 Uxbridge Road,
Ealing, London, W.5.
Filmset by Keyspools Ltd, Golborne, Lancashire.
Printed by Redwood Burn, Trowbridge and Esher.

FOREWORD

The most fervent supporters of the United Nations (UN), of which I have been one, now recognise that the political state of the world prevents that Organisation from carrying out effectively some of the peace-keeping and peace-making roles that we all hoped it would be able to perform. Despite this the member nations have failed to agree on the modifications to the Charter which are essential if it is to be made capable of discharging its most important responsibility. This is a dangerous state of affairs for the whole world. Therefore, until such a time as the necessary reforms to the UNO have been agreed, it is vitally important that we should explore other methods of resolving conflicts which endanger peace.

One such conflict which the UN has been conspicuously unsuccessful in resolving, and which everyone agrees could well endanger the peace of the world, is the dispute between Israel and its Arab neighbours. While therefore my colleagues and I on the World Security Trust were well aware that no political problem has received more concentrated attention over the past quarter of a century, it seemed to us that there were a number of factors related to the situation which had still not been faced with the necessary realism or in the necessary detail. In particular, there has been far too much generalised talk about security guarantees and far too little detailed examination of what in practice these might entail.

The plain fact is that there is going to be no peaceful settlement and therefore a continuation of the existing highly explosive situation unless and until Israel and its neighbours are convinced that any new arrangements they agree upon will provide them with a greater measure of security than they believe they have at present. Until there are proposals for a settlement which can meet this fundamental test all further negotiations are doomed to failure.

In this book David Astor and Valerie Yorke have sought to explore the means by which this increased security for all concerned might be achieved. I am convinced that their suggestions can make a most important contribution to the resolution of one of the most intractable problems of our age. It is a book which will compel people in governments and in legislatures to face up to the responsibilities and the commitments they will have to undertake, when the generalised assurances about security guarantees they say they are prepared to give come to be translated into practical actions. To some, these responsibilities and commitments may seem formidable, but I have no doubt they constitute a price all of us should be prepared to pay in order to eliminate the danger of a further conflict in the Middle East, which we all recognise could so easily bring on a much wider and more disastrous conflagration.

20 June, 1978 Harlech

CONTENTS

Sponsorship   viii

Authors' Note   x

Summary of Contents   xiii

POLITICS OF THE CONFLICT   1

1. PROPOSALS   10

2. ISRAEL'S SECURITY AND BORDERS   19

3. ROLE OF THE SUPER POWERS I: The American
Approach to Guarantees   44

4. ROLE OF THE SUPER POWERS II: 62
    i) Possibility of Joint American-Soviet Guarantees
    ii) The Forms of Super Power Cooperation

5. BORDERS: FROM SAFEGUARDS TO SECURITY
GUARANTEES   82

6. PEACE AND THE NECESSITY FOR ARMS
CONTROL   131

Appendix I: The Sinai Settlements   154

Appendix II: Maps   159

Abbreviations   171

Index   172

SPONSORSHIP

The purpose of this study is to discover what arrangements could be made and undertakings be given by 'outside' countries to increase the security of the Arab-Israeli frontiers that might be reached in a peace settlement. What those would be is assumed in this study to be approximately the frontiers of 1967, in accordance with Security Council Resolution 242.

Such a re-positioning of the present effective frontiers would mean not only new security problems for Israel: it would also mean the emergence of a political entity, either independent or linked to Jordan, of some part of former Palestine, namely the West Bank and Gaza Strip. This area would have acute problems of frontier security of its own.

The term 'security guarantees' has frequently been heard. Some writers have given it an almost magical meaning, as if it would solve these future frontier problems. Others give the term almost no meaning at all and fear it as a dangerous delusion: many Israelis take this view. But what comparatively few have done is to work out what the term could mean in practical reality, if it was internationally important to provide the service that the term implies.

The purpose of this study is to make a contribution on this front. We have paid heed to and derived benefit from our predecessors in this field. However, even when their work and ours has been put together, we recognise that it still only represents a scratching at the surface of a tough problem.

We undertook this study because the World Security Trust has long been conducting private discussions and enquiries on a question central to the affairs of our time:— how do you deal with an area of international dispute, if you cannot resolve the dispute by all-out war (because that is too dangerous), or by normal diplomacy (because the parties cannot agree) and if you cannot turn to any international agency with administrative peace-keeping capacity (because none exists)? The United Nations is still far from attaining that capacity: methods are, therefore, needed to bridge the gap until the World Body is able to do what its founders intended.

The deliberations of this small Trust have been on the basis that situations of this sort are bound to recur and that it is urgent to start devising methods of dealing with them. The Middle East has for some while offered the outstanding example of such situations: but other areas, such as North-East and Southern Africa, seem likely to produce further examples.

The World Security Trust has long favoured approaching these international problems in fundamentally the same way that the most elementary political problems have to be dealt with: that is to say, in terms of applying power in support of whatever order or agreement can be reached. It was the failure to act in this spirit on this basis and the mistaken belief in disarmament that permitted the outbreak of the Second World War.

This approach has pre-disposed us to consider the role of the most powerful states as being particularly important. We are among those who suspect that the relationship of the two so-called Super Powers contains the greatest potential both for good and for ill in matters of peace and war.

Our approach to security guarantees in the Middle East is made with no illusion that this is a simple matter nor that it is, necessarily, a problem with a solution. But we believe that this search for a method of international peace-keeping holds out at least some hope of reaching stability in the Middle East. We also believe it gives a chance of learning from the experiences of the Middle East lessons which might be of value in the next such crisis.

The members of the World Security Trust are:– Mr. David Astor; The Rt. Hon. Lord Duncan-Sandys; The Rt. Hon. Lord Gore-Booth; The Rt. Hon. Lord Harlech; Mr. Robert Stephens; Sir Edward Thompson; The Rt. Hon. Lord Thomson of Monifieth.The late Rt. Hon. John Strachey, MP was a founder member.

Authors' Note

It would be impossible to list here the many people who helped us during our visits to the Middle East, Soviet Union, United States and France with advice, facilities and hospitality. For special assistance, we would like to thank the various embassies in London and their governments, and the British Foreign and Commonwealth Office, which provided us with help throughout our journeys. Among the various libraries, we would like to thank for their help and cooperation the staffs of the International Institute for Strategic Studies and the Royal Institute of International Affairs.

We must thank all those who agreed to be interviewed and who so generously shared their views:– King Hussein and members of the Royal Diwan; the then-Minister of Defence of Israel, Shimon Peres; President Assad's political adviser, Dr. Adib Daoudi; officials at the Foreign Ministries in Egypt, Jordan, Syria and Israel; and many other officials, diplomats, politicians and academics of those countries; PLO leaders (particularly the late Said Hammami, the former PLO representative in London, for his help with introductions) and those Palestinians on the West Bank who received us in their offices and homes; officials at the State Department, National Security Council, Pentagon and members of the Sinai Field Mission; members of the various Institutes of the Academy of Sciences and officials of the Foreign Ministry in Moscow; representatives of the Quai d'Orsay in Paris and of the FCO in London; United Nations officials and their advisers, both in New York and the Middle East; and all those other officials, politicians, members of the academic community and journalists who gave us their time.

For their detailed advice and for their criticism of part or all of the early drafts, we are particularly grateful to Sydney Bailey, Christoph Bertram, François Duchêne, Lord Gore-Booth, Brigadier Michael Harbottle, Lord Harlech, Brigadier Kenneth

Hunt, Alan James, Malcolm Kerr, Keith Kyle, Colin Legum, Wolfgang Mallmann, Peter Mangold, Elizabeth Monroe, Andrew Pierre, Robert Pranger, Major-General Indar Jit Rikhye, Eric Rouleau, Ian Smart and Robert Stephens. We would also like to thank Lieutenant-General Sir Anthony Farrar-Hockley and Colonel Peter Harvey who have extended invaluable help on a personal basis. Nevertheless, the responsibility for the text lies only with the authors.

We want to thank Transworld Publishers Ltd. for the generous spirit in which they have undertaken this work and the speed of its execution.

Special thanks go to Pat Burge for her untiring help at every stage of the project and for typing most of the drafts.

Finally, the study, which was based on the past work of the World Security Trust, received the continuous support and encouragement of the Trust's members.

June 1978   David Astor
                                                          Valerie Yorke

Summary of Contents

POLITICS OF THE CONFLICT (1–9)

1. PROPOSALS (10–18)

2. ISRAEL'S SECURITY AND BORDERS

Israel's choice: whether to risk making territorial concessions on all fronts and negotiating a settlement underwritten by reliable safeguards and security guarantees with special provision for the problems of the West Bank and Gaza Strip; or whether to pursue a policy of self-maintaining defence although this would preclude a solution to the Palestinian question and is incompatible with Arab minimum demands (19–21).

Defensible Borders: The Israeli Perception: The historical development of the concept of defensible borders (21–23). The Allon Plan (23–25). Criticism on a front-by-front basis of Allon's 'strategic rationale' for an Israeli presence in occupied territory (25–33).

Self-Reliance or Dependence?: Extent of Israeli dependence on America in economic and military terms (34). Can America continue to provide Israel with such aid if Washington becomes disillusioned with Israeli policies and if this support risks antagonising America's chief oil suppliers (34–35)?

Nuclear Option: The advantages and disadvantages for Israel of turning nuclear potential into a nuclear capability (35–36).

Summary: Demographic and economic forces and their adverse effects on Israel's long-term self-defence capability (36). The concept of defensible borders and the international community (37). Bold Israeli policy over territory and Palestinian question required (38–39).

3. ROLE OF THE SUPER POWERS I:
The American Approach to Guarantees:

Given incompatibility between Israeli and Arab demands, could third parties bridge this gap by providing security guarantees (44)? What might such guarantees be and who should provide them (44–45)? American historical caution about a unilateral guarantor role (46–47).

Historical Perspective: Two forms of unilateral American guarantee: a formal defence treaty with Israel; an American guarantee of borders agreed by the two sides. Earlier proposals (46–49).

A Unilateral American Guarantee of Borders and of Demilitarisation: A unilateral American guarantee of borders unlikely to be forthcoming. 1975 Sinai Interim Agreement: a departure from previous American reluctance to accept unilateral responsibilities (49–50). Could American civilian personnel be used in a final settlement? Objections to a 'trip-wire' military presence (50–51).

A Possible Soviet Spoiler's Role: Arab insistence on Soviet participation in guarantees (51). Argument One: the Soviets as obstructionists (51–52). Argument Two: Soviets want equal role with the United States in Middle East. Soviet participation in guarantees of borders becomes *quid pro quo* for arms limitation agreements (52–53). American dilemma: Soviet involvement in peace-making process and guarantees means forfeiting benefits of unilateral diplomacy: exclusion of Soviets likely to encourage Soviet revolutionary role (53). Guarantees of borders and of demilitarisation should be multilateral (53).

An American Defence Treaty with Israel: Past official thinking circumspect. Carter Administration contemplates formal alignment on Israeli withdrawal. Possible forms of alignment (53–54). Compelling Israeli and American arguments against formal alignment (54–55). If confirmation of settlement depended on American defence treaty offer, advantages might outweigh disadvantages (55). Israeli position (56). Arab position (56). America unwilling to undertake more extensive guarantor role than necessary. Possible form: mutual defence pact (57). Provisos (57–58).

4. ROLE OF THE SUPER POWERS II :

I *POSSIBILITY OF JOINT AMERICAN-SOVIET GUARANTEES:* Necessity of involving the Soviet Union in guarantee arrangements (62–64).

Soviet Concern for Peace in the Middle East: Rejection of view that Soviet Union is interested in supporting instability in the Middle East (64–65). Historical evidence of Soviet restraint in its involvement with Arab confrontation states and PLO (65–67). Probability Soviet Union would now support a settlement (67).

Political Feasibility of Super Power Cooperation: Previous examples of cooperation (67–68). Practical difficulties of joint American–Soviet policing of a settlement or military participation in a UN force (69–70).

II *THE FORMS OF SUPER POWER COOPERATION:* Need for agreements to be endorsed by Security Council resolution (70). Such endorsement to be supplemented by multilateral political guarantees of borders and agreements (71–72).

Super Power Participation in Safeguards: Evolution of Washington's attitude to direct involvement on the ground (72–73). Soviet attitudes: acceptance of principle of demilitarised zones and guarantees (74). Soviet guarantees for Israel (75). Emphasis on the need for political parity with Washington (75–76). Elaboration on participation of Soviet observers in UN forces (76).

Summary – A Non-Combatant Super Power Role?: Feasibility of 'passive' and symbolic forms of Super Power cooperation: civilian monitoring or UN observer teams (77–78).

5. BORDERS: FROM SAFEGUARDS TO SECURITY GUARANTEES

Demilitarised Zones (DMZs): Security measures crucial to compromise (82). International consensus on their necessity (82–83). Problems differ according to which borders are involved (82–88).

I *THE SINAI AND THE GOLAN:* Political and security requirements (88–89). Proposals for extent and form of DMZs in Sinai (89–90). Golan (90–92).

United Nations: The Sinai experience (92). Security measures on a long-term basis (93). Role of UN forces in Sinai and on the Golan (93–96). Requisites for effective operations: efficient military and political command structure including proposal for a Special Representative of the Secretary General (93–94); means of ensuring quasi-permanence of forces (94); balanced and impartial forces: contingents might come from Britain, France, other West and East European states, Third World and non-aligned countries, but should exclude Super Powers except as military observers (94–96).

Verification: Ways of improving UN verification techniques (96). Importance of local party surveillance (97). Feasibility of third party tactical early warning stations on other fronts (97–98). Need for additional aerial reconnaissance (99–100).

II *THE WEST BANK AND GAZA STRIP:* Political and security requirements (100–101). Future demilitarisation of a Palestinian entity; Palestinian views on 'limitation of armaments' and international guarantees (101–103). Who would enforce armaments restrictions in a Palestinian entity and reassure Palestinians that neither Israel nor Arab states could intervene in Palestinian territory (103)?

Enforcement: A. Evolutionary Plan: Overwhelming disadvantages (103–105). *B. Innovatory Security Plan:* Establishment of a Border Guard astride the Israeli–Palestinian frontier and along the Jordan River (105–106). Tasks (106–107). Necessity for a new international institution: a Middle East Control Commission (107–108). Form and composition of Border Guard (109). Mandate (109). Location and technical feasibility of guarantor operations (110). Surveillance (111–112). Open Borders (113).

III *JERUSALEM* (113).

IV *THE LEBANON:* Political and security requirements (113–115). Buffer zone (115–116). Enforcement (116–118). UNIFIL precedent (118). Border Guard approach (118). Tasks (119). Authority and Operational Principles (119).

Border Guard Versus UN: Advantages (120).

V *THE ROLE OF OUTSIDE PRESSURE:* As back-bone of border agreements (120). Need for neutral international body under UN auspices to identify aggressor (121). UN umpire role, intervention and procedures (121). Need for multilateral sanctions and guarantees if UN procedures fail (122). Super Power cooperation and 'agreed ground rules' for implementation of sanctions (122).

6. PEACE AND THE NECESSITY FOR ARMS CONTROL

Basic difficulties and possible forms. Emphasis on the need for a suppliers' agreement. Dangers of a continuation of the current arms race (131–133).

Political Feasibility of Suppliers' Cooperation in Arms Control: Respective attitudes. France (135), Britain (135–136), the Soviet Union (136). Need for an American initiative with Soviet cooperation (136–137).

The Form of Arms Control: The relative ineffectiveness of earlier attempts in the absence of a settlement. The possibility of a suppliers' agreement along the lines of the Tripartite Declaration (137–139). Need for the chief suppliers to agree jointly on restrictions on sales and transfers of arms and advanced technology (139). Possible forms of cooperation; proposal for informal approach on the lines of London nuclear suppliers club taking the form of a Permanent Standing Arms Control Committee of the four chief suppliers; Super Powers as Co-Chairmen; all Middle East states ideally to be represented. In effect, Committee to provide diplomatic forum for Super Powers and secondary suppliers to coordinate arms trade policies (139–141).

Arms Transfer Restrictions: Types of restrictions: i) arms transfers to confrontation states by suppliers external to the region: need for both quantitative and qualitative restrictions; complex problems of assuring military 'balance' (141–143); ii) arms transfers from non-confrontation to confrontation states: possibility of applying sanctions against non-confrontation states that violate arms transfer agreements (143–144); iii) indigenous arms production: need for suppliers to agree on limitations on arms technology transfers (144).

A Permanent Standing Arms Control Committee (PSACC): Verification and enforcement of agreements by PSACC requires supervisory machinery. Means of verification include possibility of inspection points or a check-on-challenge procedure (144–145). Need to adjust arms control measures to meet changing security situations (145). Need to develop a range of potential sanctions including, at the extreme, denial of other arms permitted under agreement or compensatory deliveries to the 'threatened' state (146–147).

The Recipients' Contribution: Possibility of complementary agreements between recipient states; voluntary agreement not to seek to breach suppliers' restrictions on arms imports. Limitation of the value of recipient agreements (147–148).

Summary: Arms control key to security system. Political feasibility of arms control measures. A new departure in the détente process at the regional level (149).

POLITICS OF THE CONFLICT
New Kind of War

The Middle East war has been one of a new kind that may become a familiar kind: a war between relatively small states which acquire the backing of the Super Powers.

This support, naturally, raises the level of armaments far above the means of the states doing the fighting. And so, although the direction of the war may remain nominally with the combatant states, the Super Powers inevitably acquire a high degree of control. It is only a negative control, the power to restrain or stop the fighting. But it introduces a two-tier command of strategy that is new in the history of warfare and has unfamiliar implications.

In such wars, the interests of the local states and those of their backers, the Super Powers, are not identical. The local states want a decisive win, a victory that will give them the territory and frontiers they claim: they therefore must want whatever arms are needed for that purpose. But the supporting Super Powers, no matter how deeply they are committed to the defence of their protégés, are always hesitant to introduce arms that might be used for an attempted knock-out.

This reluctance is based on rational self-interest. Just as each Super Power knows that, if his protégé is threatened with defeat, he may have to increase his commitment and, possibly, even send in his own troops, so each has come to realise that this is equally true of the other Super Power. The most famous lesson for the United States in this respect came when General MacArthur overran North Korea and brought the weight of the Chinese Army (then supported by the Soviets) in against him. The consequence was an acute risk of world war.

The Middle East has produced similar experiences. The Yom Kippur attack of 1973 immediately forced the United States to use its own 'planes to fly in military supplies: then, when the Israelis crossed the Canal and threatened Cairo with disaster, it was the Soviets who called on the Israelis to withdraw and reinforced their

1

demand by mobilising their own airborne divisions. Washington countered with a Nuclear Alert: but the Israelis were obliged to pull back. Both Super Powers had been reminded of the dangers of a decisive victory by their protégés.

This was not a unique episode. The Israelis had been similarly recalled when they reached the Canal in 1956. On other occasions, they were prevented by their advisers from moving on Damascus – always because a decisive success might have obliged the Soviets to intervene.

A precisely parallel restriction has been imposed on the Arab states. Whenever they have asked for the means to attack Israeli cities, this has been refused them. The main cause of Egypt's break with Moscow was, indeed, Soviet reluctance to supply powerful offensive weapons. And the Soviets have always been cautious for exactly the same reason as have the Americans. Arab attacks on Israeli cities might have compelled the Americans to permit counter-attacks on Cairo – with the obvious risk of an escalation towards world war.

Indeed, the Super Powers have been more than cautious in the Middle East: they have discreetly worked together to restrict the war. Notably, they together negotiated and voted in the United Nations for a Cease Fire Resolution in the worst days of 1973. The Soviets also made at that time their suggestion for joint American–Soviet patrols to police a cease-fire in Sinai.

New Kind of Peace

This two-tier control of the war has already produced two unprecedented results. First, the local parties have become undefeatable. Battles between them can be won; but if either local party looks like winning the war, both Super Powers will move to prevent that happening – for fear that this could involve them in an escalation.

Second, this stalemate means there can be no normal peace conference. A peace conference has, normally, been an occasion when the winners invite the losers to discuss the conditions of a settlement. Whose wishes shall prevail has already been decided on the battle-field. In contrast, a peace conference between the Middle East combatants would be a deadlocked meeting of undefeated parties with unresolved grievances. A resolution of their major differences must obviously involve some security concessions by one side. But why should such concessions be made? Left to themselves, there is no good reason why undefeated combatant states should make major concessions. It seems likely that fundamental issues left over by a stalemated war can only be brought to a settlement by the wish and commitment of the supporting Powers which have created the stalemate.

And there are, of course, major issues to be settled; notably, the awkward, central question of the rights of the Palestinians. The original object of this war for the Arab nations was to restore to the Palestinians something of what they had lost. But the hard fact is that geography makes it genuinely difficult to do this without endangering Israel.

This is not at all surprising, since in size and form the struggle which broke out within Palestine in 1947 was a civil war – a struggle between two loosely-organised communities living within one area of government, both claiming sovereignty over the same territory and both determined to hold the capital city. Its upshot was a division of farming areas, the road-system, the capital city itself by a partition line that was never militarily defensible from either side.

Historical Accident

These events occurred at a convulsive moment of world history. The founding of Israel and disappearance of Palestine chanced to happen when Asia and Africa were beginning to send home their European colonial settlers. The Arab countries, being part of this movement, saw the Zionists as an untimely wave of colonists comparable to the Italians in Libya or the French in Algeria. Zionists found this hard to understand: and it was, indeed, a totally unrelated accident that the horrific treatment of the European Jews which compelled the creation of Israel coincided with this awakening of the subordinated peoples of Asia and Africa. But it was this awakening that made the displacement of the Palestinians so significant to the Third World and still makes their cause one that cannot be dismissed.

The struggle with the Palestinians remains the most intense part

3

of the Arab–Israeli conflict. Moreover, the Palestinian-inhabited areas of the West Bank and Gaza Strip are so physically close to Israel's centres of population that very few Israelis favour letting those areas out of their own military control. Nor would they want the United Nations to patrol frontiers between themselves and the Palestinians. Israelis know that forces representing the UN do not normally undertake duties that may involve killing or being killed; but Israelis believe that someone must accept these harsh possibilities – if Israeli families are not to live in constant danger. So they intend to keep these areas demilitarised themselves.

Here is a situation where, if the parties are asked to find a solution unaided, none is likely to be found. The Israelis, to safeguard their most vital interests, will want to stay as the military overlords of some one-and-a-half million Palestinians in all. The Palestinians will not accept this tutelage willingly. And the rest of the Arab world will look on, much as Africans watch Rhodesia and South Africa, unable to settle down with the subjection of their fellows.

The Israeli demand for security and the Palestinian demand for self-determination are equally passionately held and the truth is that there is no peaceful settlement in sight. But if none is found, matters will not stay still. There will be trouble inside those Arab states whose governments have put their hopes in the United States. There will be a further radicalisation of the PLO: anti-Western and particularly anti-American hatred will be transmitted wherever there are Palestinian workers. A revolutionary ferment in the Middle East might ultimately make it impossible for the Soviets to align themselves with the United States in any peace settlement.

This is so serious a situation that it is necessary to speak frankly, even at the risk of offending the susceptibilities of those who have held the military and diplomatic initiative in the Middle East in these years, the Americans and, in a junior role, the Israelis. In implying that their policies are dangerously stuck, no lack of respect or of sympathy for either of them is intended. It is, however, inappropriate to be mealy-mouthed if the dangers ahead are as great as they appear. And it is, of course, useless to criticise unless some alternative course can be suggested.

What has really gone wrong? What have been the mistaken assumptions? How could more successful policies be developed?

4

Propositions

1. Everybody has behaved as if the Middle East states were as genuinely sovereign as, say, France and Prussia in the nineteenth century – while the United States government has known from its supportive actions how deep has been the dependence of these states either on itself or the Soviet Union. This tactfulness has obscured the responsibility of the supporting Powers for bringing about peace. It has been wrongly made to appear, even to the American public, that this responsibility rested primarily with Israel and the Arab states.

2. Israel's heroic wish for military self-reliance, coming from the harsh Jewish experience of centuries of dependence, has led Israelis to develop some war aims that are inherently impossible. Yet, successive United States governments have not (or, but seldom) reminded the Israelis publicly that their aim of extended 'defensible frontiers', far from bringing them greater independence, must condemn them to permanent enmity with their neighbours and a continued need of massive, perhaps growing, military support. Washington's natural hope that Israel would one day cease to be a defence risk, threatening their own involvement, evidently led American official thinking to accept in general terms the aim that Israel would eventually have normal, secure frontiers – although it was never explained how this could possibly accord with even minimum Palestinian demands.

3. For a quarter-century, American statesmen and diplomats (and those of other Western states) have cut themselves off from any first-hand contact with Palestinians: their consequent insensitivity to that side of the problem has become a self-imposed handicap.

4. When the Palestinian issue crystallised as a widely-supported proposal for an independent West Bank-cum-Gaza 'entity', the Israelis at once made it clear that this would threaten their security. Some Arab statesmen wondered why the United States could not offer Israel a bilateral guarantee to encourage it to make peace. But American policy-makers had long known that there was no chance of Congress ever agreeing to an American bilateral guarantee of Israel's frontiers – until *after* a comprehensive

5

settlement. The difference between these two approaches to guarantees was only discussed in learned journals and the argument for guarantees *before* a settlement was seldom made publicly plain.

5. One reason for this silence has been that the Israelis themselves have not asked for guarantees *before* a peace settlement (since Ben Gurion's efforts to obtain alliances in the 1950s). They have come to think that this would weaken their bargaining position and oblige them in advance to accept the borders that would be guaranteed. They have also come to believe that it serves their interests best to leave their all-important military relations with America on the basis of a moral obligation and that any contractual agreement might restrict America's real commitment: further, that a formal arrangement of this sort would reduce Israel's tactical freedom to act. They have, therefore, treated 'guarantees' with reserve, almost as a taboo-subject that could not be usefully discussed until after a peace settlement has somehow been reached – with terms sufficiently favourable to themselves that guarantees of their frontiers would have become relatively unnecessary, the 'icing on the cake'.

6. Washington has been well-pleased not to be asked to give Israel guarantees. No way has been found in which Washington could formally underwrite Israel's territorial safety without risking a Vietnam-type commitment. Inviting the Soviets to join in a peace treaty that would include various forms of guarantee has been the theme of former Under Secretary of State, Mr. George Ball: but his has remained a lonely voice. For many years, it has suited the convenience both of American and of Israeli governments to leave this question of guarantees almost undiscussed, except in academic circles. Even there, the American discussion has often been vitiated by unconsciously treating Israeli anxieties as more important than Arab sentiments.

7. It is said that American governments are unable to go against the so-called American Jewish 'lobby': but this is an exaggeration. The circumstances when Israel's American supporters can win powerful sympathy from the general public and limit government action are, very properly, when the State of Israel seems to be in danger. So, if Washington wishes to persuade Israel to withdraw from the West Bank, the American public must see that this request does not mean endangering a much-admired small country. If that assurance should require an American committment on the ground, possibly in association with the Soviet Union, then the American public is going to need time to accept this prospect. Future American–Israeli relations may depend on having all these matters out in public discussion, frankly and courageously, now.

8. Successive American Administrations have, in fact, sought to provide safety for Israel simply by arming that country highly; and this continues to be the chief method. This has been the expression of Washington's hope to make Israel apparently self-supporting in defence. The policy has, of course, had some success; but it shows no sign of achieving stability. Essentially, it means fuelling an arms race in a small, contested area. Moreover, heavy arms have no relevance to preventing guerrilla action from the West Bank, which would be the most difficult security problem in any politically-acceptable peace.

9. A few people still think that the United States could maintain peace in the Middle East by itself. There is, unfortunately, little basis for believing this. America's best efforts to regulate the affair between its own allies, Turkey and Greece, over Cyprus have shown the limits of alliance-control. Nor have the Soviets been able to control relations peacefully in their area of solo-power, the Horn of Africa. It is a mistake to think of the capacity of a Super Power to stop wars even between dependent nations in terms of an old-style empire's ability to keep peace within its domains. Only in situations of direct control, such as the Soviets have in Eastern Europe, can a Super Power exercise anything resembling imperial authority. In other international situations, the Super Powers have been effective as peace-keepers only in those few cases where they have been able to act together in some measure of agreement, i.e. across Europe and in the Middle East during the cease-fires of 1956 and 1973, for example.

10. If American hegemony in the Middle East is a fantasy, so is the talk of 'bringing in' or of 'allowing' the Soviets to take part in its affairs. The Soviets live in the near-neighbourhood; have a naval fleet to its east and west; have supplied about half the arms in the area until recently; and there are Soviet staff officers operating by invitation in southern Arabia and north-east Africa. The Soviet Union can, therefore, supply the military needs of any Middle Eastern state as quickly as can the United States: and none of these states, including Egypt, needs to be reminded of this fact.

Super Power Relations

To conclude. There is no sign of the Arab–Israeli conflict being ended by an agreement between the combatants. As this war has been, in the arms used, one between the United States and Soviet Union, the only stable peace must be one that both these Powers accept.

Proposals for such a peace settlement are examined in the following pages. These take into consideration the interests and feelings of the local parties in all the main issues. It is, however, necessary first to ask whether cooperation between the Super Powers to the extent required for such a peace settlement is a possibility. Some would even question whether such cooperation between them is desirable.

Some people believe that one or other of the Super Powers represents evil incarnate, as did Hitler's Germany. To those who regard either the United States or the Soviet Union with this kind of mistrust, any cooperation between them must be anathema. Others have a generalised fear that cooperation between the Super Powers might produce an overwhelming concentration of power in the world and that this could become the embryo of a world dictatorship. Yet others have the opposite view: that no cooperation between the Super Powers is ever going to be possible and that this inability is going to lead to the world's ruin.

Without seeking to resolve these contradictory opinions – all of which may contain a scintilla of truth – it is platitudinous to assert that the peace of the world is likely to depend on whether the forces, rational or irrational, that drive the Super Powers into conflict become stronger than those that enable them to work together.

It also seems probable that the present phase of world politics is going to increase the mutual mistrust between the Super Powers and might even lead to active hostility. The continent of Africa seems destined to see as dangerous a rivalry between them as was played out at the beginning of this century in the Balkan peninsula between the Great Powers of that time. With the West lumbered with its historic, commercial associations with South Africa; and with the Soviets playing the role of champions of radical black nationalism, which the Chinese would like to take from them, a disastrous collision seems more than a possibility.

The importance of the Middle East in this connection could be decisive. If no peace is now reached and the area returns to a seething conflict backed by the Super Powers (with Egypt perhaps joining Israel and Saudi Arabia in an anti-Soviet alignment) then this could lead to an extension of an 'ideological' Middle Eastern war into the various current African struggles.

On the other hand, if a Middle East peace, based on recognition of the obvious common self-interest of the Super Powers in avoiding world war, could be set up, a new process might be started. There would be nothing easy in extending any such agreements to other local wars. No single formula would apply to all situations and, certainly, the complete prevention of local wars would never be possible. Moreover, those who regard the South African dictatorship, for instance, as a political monstrosity that is not likely to be reformed without the use of some external force would not consider the prevention of all local wars to be morally desirable.

What the lessons of the Middle East might be able to teach is only this:– how an international system, based on Super Power cooperation, might be able to contain local convulsions and prevent them leading to world war. It is a question of whether the wish to survive of the Super Powers (not their virtue or wisdom or brotherly love) can build a working connection between them capable of restricting their own rivalry and of preventing the quarrels of smaller powers from leading them along suicidal courses.

D.A.

1. PROPOSALS

Timing
1. If the Super Powers are to take an initiative in creating a Middle East Peace, they must find a way of accommodating Israeli and Arab anxieties *before* peace is negotiated. In particular, Washington should discard the orthodoxy that guarantees should *supplement* a negotiated settlement and spell out the form that safeguards and guarantees might take *before* negotiations (38–39).

Framework
2. In conformity with the wide international consensus, a comprehensive Middle East Peace Treaty would be based on UN Security Council Resolutions 242 and 338 and on the creation of a Palestinian 'homeland' on the West Bank and Gaza Strip (19).

3. The political framework for an international endorsement of that Peace Treaty would be a resolution of the Security Council (71).

4. In order to meet Israeli and Palestinian and other Arab security requirements, the Peace Treaty should include a Security Plan. This should:
  i) provide security assurances for Israel to withdraw to approximate 1967 borders (38);
  ii) provide security for a future Palestinian entity, whatever its constitutional form; and for Israel's neighbouring Arab states (38).

International Agreements
5. Under the Peace Treaty, there would therefore need to be international agreements for:
  i) demilitarised zones (DMZs) astride all Israel's frontiers with at least a token strip on Israeli territory (89–92, 101–103, 115–116);

10

ii) UN peace-keeping forces and local early warning stations on Israel's borders with Egypt, Syria and, possibly, the Lebanon (but see 113–120) for a period of at least fifteen years (92–96, 97);

iii) an international guarantor force (Border Guard) with a special mandate under the Peace Treaty to use force, stationed for an indefinite period on both sides of the border of a new Palestinian entity (West Bank and Gaza Strip), astride the Israeli–Lebanese border and in areas south of the Litani River (106, 119);

iv) involvement of the United States and Soviet Union in a non-combatant capacity in the provision of ground surveillance and aerial reconnaissance on all borders of Israel and of the Palestinian entity (72, 97–100, 112);

v) formal multilateral political guarantees would be undertaken independently of the UN by the United States and Soviet Union and other powers, either together or separately, to guarantee both the DMZs and borders of Israel and neighbouring states, including the new Palestinian entity and the other agreements reached under the Peace Treaty. Signatories would undertake to impose within 'agreed ground rules' economic and military sanctions against violators, aimed at restoring the *status quo ante*. The implementation of sanctions would depend on the principle that the Super Powers could be expected to support their respective clients if these latter were threatened, but to desist from doing so if their clients sought to upset the *status quo* (71–72, 122–123);

vi) a Permanent Standing Arms Control Committee (PSACC) of supplier and recipient states would be set up to maintain a military balance between Israel and its neighbouring states, and perhaps later on of other states in the region (140, 144–147, 149).

Bilateral Guarantees

6. An American–Israeli mutual defence pact, for instance, and similar formal Soviet guarantees might also be undertaken if the countries involved so wish, in addition to the above, to provide gaurantees of 'last resort' for the secutity of the countries concerned (53–57, 91, 92, 123).

11

BORDERS

7. The frontiers to be established (approximately those of 1967) with minor reciprocal rectifications would require varying systems of guarantees in which the Super Powers should be involved: the fact is that only their involvement could make the guarantees sufficiently reliable to make the parties reach a compromise.

Egypt and Syria

8. The Egyptian and Syrian borders with Israel, having dividing geographical features (deserts, hills) and no overlapping populations, could be treated as normal inter-state borders; that is, the parties would depend, mainly, on their own national forces for their defence. The additional security arrangements would be those already existing in Sinai:– DMZs with UN troops, local surveillance stations and Super Power civilian-manned monitoring stations and air reconnaissance providing an early warning system against surprise attack (83–84, 89–100).

9. This would be supplemented by the formal multilateral guarantees undertaken by the Super Powers and other powers to guarantee the DMZs and borders (71–72).

Palestinian Entity

10. The borders around the West Bank and Gaza Strip would have neither geographical features nor differentiated populations. Moreover, as the new Palestinian entity would be virtually demilitarised under a Peace Treaty, there could be no defence by national forces for it. The Jordanian forces could provide no protection, being too weak for credibility against Israeli incursions (86–87, 100–103).

11. Correspondingly, Israel, within its 1967 borders, could not protect itself from Palestinian guerrillas – unless there was military control of the West Bank and Gaza Strip and an active policing of all their borders. This has been the essence of the Allon, Dayan and Begin proposals; but their plans are not politically acceptable to the Arabs. The question from the Israeli perspective is, therefore, whether any international security system could provide similar protection (87–88, 100–103).

12. Securing a border between communities claiming each other's land requires special arrangements. A workable security system would therefore depend on two conditions to be agreed by Israelis, Palestinians and Jordanians:

i) except for light weapons for an internal security force (a Palestinian Army), no arms would be permitted inside a Palestinian entity established on the West Bank and Gaza Strip (100, 106);

ii) apart from this single limitation on their sovereignty, Palestinians should enjoy complete self-government immediately upon the signing of a Peace Treaty (101, 102, 106).

13. Some suggested requirements of the security system for the frontiers of a new Palestinian entity are:

i) an international guarantor force (Border Guard) would be stationed around the frontiers of a Palestinian entity and along its internal connecting corridor: it would also patrol the Jordan River frontier, whether the Palestinian entity and Jordan were politically linked or not (106, 113);

ii) the tasks of the Border Guard would be:
   a) to prevent terrorist raids and reprisals from either side;
   b) to seal Palestinian frontiers against the entry of illegal arms;

and, c) to confiscate any weapons that may escape detection at the frontier (106);

iii) the Border Guard and Palestinian internal security force would cooperate in investigating alleged breaches of the peace agreements occurring on Palestinian territory. But if the Palestinian authorities wished to reduce their involvement, the Border Guard would carry out the necessary inspection with whatever degree of cooperation it was extended. The Border Guard (or, alternatively, a special force maintained for this purpose) would also be empowered to apprehend and disarm offenders on Palestinian territory. To preserve good relations with the Palestinian authorities, all offenders would be handed back to their respective political authority after being disarmed (107);

iv) any Israeli offenders against the Treaty provisions who were caught by the Border Guard in the DMZs would be handed back to their national authority (107);

v) to carry out these tasks, the Border Guard would require a mandate to use the amount of force necessary for its purposes over an indefinite period of time. As it is unlikely that this could be obtained under UN auspices and as all parties in Israel express distrust of the UN, the mandate would have to be given under the Treaty (108, 109);

vi) initially, there would be no open Israeli–Palestinian frontier, but only a limited number of crossing-points, as at present along the Jordan River. Progressive relaxation should be made in the control of movement across a Palestinian entity's frontiers, but only as and when all the local parties agreed (113);

vii) the security system would continue until Israel, Jordan and the new Palestinian entity all agreed otherwise (108);

14. The outline of a possible organisation for ensuring demilitarisation of the West Bank and Gaza Strip and token strips of Israel and Jordan, and for the protection of the Palestinian entity and its neighbours is:

i) an international Control Commission created under a Middle East Peace Treaty and registered with the UN; its constitutional status would be comparable to that of other security organisations set up under treaties, e.g. North Atlantic Treaty Organisation (NATO) (108);

ii) it would consist of all the Treaty signatories, the United States and Soviet Union (who would be Co-Chairmen), West and East European states, and other states prepared to support a Middle East peace and resulting agreements. It would have a politically-balanced representation and all members would have to be approved by Israel, its neighbours and by the Super Powers (108–109);

iii) it would be financed by its members according to their means: it might also be supported by the oil-producing states and oil-using states (e.g. Japan) which profit from peace in the Middle East (109);

iv) it would have a Secretary General and Secretariat, perhaps based at Geneva (108–109);

v) it would authorise, recruit and maintain the Border Guard with a mandate to carry out the above tasks (108);

vi) the Border Guard's Commander would come from a non-aligned state; all military and civil staff and national contingents would be seconded from their national forces and would come under the Commission's authority. National contingents could *not* come from the Super Powers, Middle East states or from states unacceptable to Israel, Jordan or the new Palestinian entity (109). But all contingents would need to be militarily qualified to fulfil active service tasks and be recruited from states willing to commit their contingents to the full operational hazards of the Border Guard (109);

vii) the Border Guard would have jurisdiction, under the Treaty, over strips of ground parallel with the frontiers of five hundred metres width on each side of the frontier, i.e. a total width of one thousand metres. This to extend around the Israeli–Palestinian frontiers and along the Jordan River. The 500-metre strips would be taken equally from Israel, the Palestinian entity and Jordan. Each party would cede irreversibly to the Control Commission the right to use such strips and also the right to control access to any air-strips needed by the Border Guard outside the frontier strips. The width of the strips proposed would permit Border Guard operations to continue from one side of the frontier only, if one national party withdrew its cooperation (110–111, 157);

viii) the Border Guard would consist of lightly-armed infantry with light missiles and armoured personnel carriers (APCs) and would have air support. It would be based on and be provisioned from the British base at Akrotiri in Cyprus, which would be lent for the purpose. Maintenance of the Border Guard would be done by light aircraft from Akrotiri to air-strips in or near the requisitioned frontier strips (111);

ix) the Border Guard would require between five and ten thousand men – numbers depending on whether small border rectifications for ease of monitoring are possible and whether the Border Guard and monitoring teams are equipped with the most advanced technology (111);

x) a surveillance system to monitor and verify military activities would be established under the authority of the Control Commission around the Israeli–Palestinian borders and along the Jordan River. It would consist of unmanned sensors watch stations and on-site inspection teams, and would ideally be located in the frontier strips (111–112);

15

xi) monitoring teams would consist of an equal representation of Western and Communist countries and of some non-aligned states (112);

xii) as on the other fronts, the role of the United States and Soviet Union would be strictly non-combatant. They would co-chair the Control Commission and relate its activities to those of the PSACC, i.e. see that, eventually, the Border Guard could not be challenged without immediate consequences to the attacker in the form of sanctions. But conspicuous Super Power support for the whole security system would be an essential deterrent factor. By participating in monitoring, as separate teams operating within the frontier strips, and by providing aerial reconnaissance, finance and logistic support, the Super Powers could demonstrate their commitment to the Border Guard to the full; but their personnel would not come under the Force Commander, nor could they instruct him except through the Control Commission (112);

Jerusalem

15. West Bank and Gaza Strip security measures could be adopted in Jerusalem whatever the political future of the city:

   i) all Jerusalem could be demilitarised;
   ii) Border Guard units could be stationed at sensitive points under the authority of the Control Commission;
   iii) Israel and the Palestinians could share civilian policing functions in the Holy Places;

but, iv) they would police separately those areas over which Israel and the Palestinian entity respectively have administrative and political control (113).

Lebanon

16. On this northern frontier, the problem is not so much the threat of surprise attack on Israel by Lebanon or *vice versa*. This is because Lebanon has not behaved as a confrontation state, and because the Lebanese and Israeli armies could be separated to supply early warning (time and space) (31).

17. However, because many Palestinians may choose to live in south Lebanon after a peace settlement and will therefore be living

16

side-by-side with Israelis, parts of the Israeli–Lebanese border may need to be controlled in the same way as the Palestinian entity's borders (115). This would depend on whether or not the Lebanese Army could assert its authority over south Lebanon. If not, then Border Guard contingents, stationed astride parts of the Israeli–Lebanese border and in the Palestinian-inhabited areas of south Lebanon, would come under the authority of the Middle East Control Commission (119).

18. In terms of form, composition and mandate, the Border Guard in Lebanon would resemble its counter-part on the West Bank and Gaza Strip, and would carry out similar tasks (119).

ARMS CONTROL

19. Middle East wars have been partly contained by Super Power restraint in supplying arms; the key to an enduring peace would be a similar willingness to control arms supplies. This is because Super Power support for arms control would be linked by the Peace Treaty agreements to Super Power visible support of international forces and safeguards in DMZs and to Super Power guarantees of frontiers: any local state threatening another with force would be challenging its own material backer (149).

20. Not only must the present arms levels be lowered: a balance must be kept in a complex of relationships. This would be an unprecedented enterprise requiring agreement on arms transfers to the region as a whole. Its chances of success would depend on there being an understanding between the rival Super Powers that cooperation over arms control in this area was in their own self-interest (139–140).

21. The instrument of control of exports of conventional arms and technology would be the PSACC of the four principal supplier states; it would be set up under the Peace Treaty, with the Super Powers acting as Co-Chairmen; its membership would have to be agreed at the peace conference and would need to include the recipient states negotiating the peace settlement as well as the chief arms suppliers (140).

22. The Committee's functions would be a) to establish what should be the (no doubt, varying) level of arms of each Middle East state required for its security (131); b) to coordinate the policies of the main arms suppliers and to regulate arms transfers accordingly (141–144); c) to check the implementation of arms transfer restrictions; and, d) to exercise sanctions against states violating agreements and/or guarantees to act in support of a state under threat (144–147).

23. Although without precedent, a Super Power role in monitoring Middle East stability along these lines would reduce Super Power military competition and the likelihood of confrontation – and would represent a major step towards institutionalising détente at the regional level (149).

THE UNITED NATIONS ROLE:
A RECAPITULATION

24. Peace-keeping operations along the Israeli frontiers with Egypt and Syria would (it is proposed) have the same constitutional relationship to the United Nations as have the present peace-keeping operations in these areas. However, it is proposed that two other fields of peace-keeping:

    i) the method of controlling the frontiers and demilitari-sation of areas where Palestinians live beside Israelis,

and, ii) the arms control system for the whole region

should be the responsibility of *ad hoc* bodies set up under a Middle East Peace Treaty, which would only be registered with the United Nations and possibly observed by UN liaison officers. The reasons for this are:–

    i) these tasks require a degree of freedom and speed of executive action that is beyond the possibility of present UN procedures, but might be possible for a group of states agreed on a limited, specific purpose;

    ii) the Israelis' lack of confidence in the political impartiality of the UN towards themselves, as well as in the UN's capacity to act; they would not agree to place themselves under its protection.

2. ISRAEL'S SECURITY AND BORDERS

The only internationally-accepted framework for Middle East negotiations on the border issue is still UN Security Council Resolutions 242 (November 1967) and 338 (October 1973).[1] In addition, there now exists a wide international consensus that a Palestinian 'homeland' should be created on the West Bank and Gaza Strip.[2] Resolution 242 recognises the inadmissibility of the acquisition of territory by conquest and calls for 'withdrawal of Israeli armed forces from territories occupied in the recent conflict'. It also notes the right of every state in the area to live within 'secure and recognized borders'. In doing so, it recognises the necessity 'for guaranteeing the territorial inviolability and political independence of every state in the area, through measures including the establishment of demilitarized zones'. The key questions, then, are: how to render secure approximate 1967 borders, particularly Israel's border with a new Palestinian 'homeland' (whatever its constitutional form and whether or not it has links with Jordan) and where to locate the demilitarised zones (DMZs)?

Israel has argued that withdrawal from territories (as opposed to *the* territories) implies *partial* withdrawal and has stressed that there is no *a priori* obligation, on anyone's part, to return to the 1949 armistice lines.[3] This, Israeli officialdom has insisted in the past, does not reflect a desire for territorial expansion, or ideological and historical motivation (though the Likud claims Judaea, Samaria and the Gaza Strip as part of the homeland promised by God to the people of Israel); rather, it is because the 1949 lines lack legal validity as political frontiers and are also militarily indefensible. The official view is that defensible borders would provide Israel with a measure of strategic depth and with lines of topographical and strategic importance, thereby reducing the temptation of Arab attack; provide early air alert; decrease the likelihood of infiltration and diminish the possibility of economic

19

harassment – either a diversion of the source of the Jordan River or a blockade at Sharm-el-Shaikh.

Israel's most recent elaboration of its demand for defensible borders has been Prime Minister Begin's Plan for yielding sovereignty over Sinai whilst maintaining special arrangements there for civilian settlements and military air-fields. There would be limited 'self-rule' for the Palestinians on the West Bank and Gaza Strip with Israel retaining responsibility for security and public order.[4] This Plan is quite incompatible with Palestinian and other Arab minimum requirements: those Arab states which have accepted Resolution 242 demand *full* withdrawal from all lands occupied since June 1967 and the right of Palestinians to self-determination, including the possible establishment of an independent state. They point out that Israeli security ultimately depends on a peace acceptable to Arabs and Palestinians, rather than on Israeli occupation of territory. And the Palestine Liberation Organisation (PLO), officially recognised at Rabat in October 1974 as the 'sole legitimate representative' of the Palestinian people, demands self-determination – the right to establish a national authority on the West Bank and Gaza Strip in the event of Israeli withdrawal from these two parts of Palestine.[5] In short, Israel's security demands preclude a solution to the Palestinian question; and without a solution to this crucial issue, there can be no comprehensive settlement.

By separating out the security and territorial issues, President Carter has tried to bridge this gap between the Israeli security requirement and the Arab and Palestinian political ones: he has said that Israel will have to withdraw from nearly all territory occupied in 1967, with only minor adjustments to armistice lines. He sugared this particular pill by distinguishing between legal and recognised borders approximating 1967 borders, and defence lines. These latter, he suggested, should be situated beyond the legal borders for an interim period.[6] In other words, Israel's need for security (particularly in connection with the West Bank) was recognised, but it was suggested that this might be provided by other than a purely Israeli presence.

The Israeli Government, therefore, has a choice of strategies on the border issue: i) to offer territorial and political concessions on all fronts and a negotiated settlement underwritten by what this paper argues might be reliable safeguards and external guarantees, with special provision for the unique problems of the West Bank and Gaza Strip; ii) to pursue a security policy based on self-maintaining defence involving minimum territorial concessions; or, iii) to opt for a combination of these, possibly along the lines of the Allon or Begin Plans. It is argued by Israel that this last option would permit it to look after its own security on the West Bank and Gaza Strip.

To take the last two options first, consideration of three important elements of present Israeli security policy – defensible borders, self-reliance and a potential nuclear capability – suggest that serious questions could be raised about the viability of Israeli strategy. This is because such a policy would not permit the negotiation of a peace acceptable to Arabs and Palestinians, and a continuation of the *status quo* is likely to end in another war with the use of more devastating weapons. While the policy could provide Israel with the self-maintaining defence of its borders that it seeks for some years, it could not do so indefinitely as some Israelis believe. Eventually, therefore, Israel might be encouraged to opt openly for a nuclear deterrent. Inevitably, the price of such self-delusion would mean increasing isolation from the world in political and economic terms. For it is unlikely that America would wish to continue its close association with Israel if the latter adopted a nuclear strategy. As it is, Israel has already developed some features of a garrison state: in 1976, total emigration exceeded immigration.

Defensible Borders: The Israeli Perception

The concept of 'secure or defensible' borders emerged after the Six Day War. On 12 June 1967, Prime Minister Levi Eshkol said that Israel wanted a formal and binding peace treaty arrived at in direct negotiations with the Arab states – a treaty incorporating the acceptance of 'secure, agreed and recognized boundaries'. Israel would not return to the pre-1967 territorial situation.[7] But where were these boundaries to be?

After the 1967 war, Israel contemplated complete withdrawal except from Jerusalem, which it had annexed, and possibly from the Golan Heights. This position hardened following the August 1967 Khartoum Arab Summit Conference. By 1969, the Israeli Labour Party reached consensus on territory to be retained: namely,

21

Jerusalem, the Golan Heights, the Gaza Strip, Sharm-el-Shaikh and a corridor to it from Eilat. Yigal Allon and Moshe Dayan produced plans for the West Bank: Allon suggested the creation of an Israeli-occupied military zone along the Jordan River, and Dayan proposed setting up military posts along the hill crest of Judaea and Samaria. But an official initiative over the territorial issue proved impossible due to leadership divisions over the best policy to pursue.[8]

The effect of Jarring's Aide Mémoire of February 1971 was to make the Israeli Government go public on its demands concerning borders.[9] Fearing that Jarring was seeking to press Israel into forfeiting geographical security in exchange for uncertain security guarantees, Mrs. Golda Meir, then Prime Minister, outlined Israel's bargaining terms. These included the retention of Sharm-el-Shaikh, the Golan Heights, Jerusalem and part of the West Bank; demilitarisation of Sinai would be supervised by a mixed force which must include Israeli and perhaps Egyptian troops.[10]

A statement published two days earlier reflected the tenets of defensible borders on which Mrs. Meir's position was based. Israel would resist pressure that aimed at resurrecting Israel's past 'territorial vulnerability': withdrawal would be possible only to boundaries that were geographically secure. Thus, Israel would not surrender a location such as Sharm-el-Shaikh to the protection of international agreements which by their very substance could only be tenuous. After three wars, Israel had the right to maintain with its own forces the security of Sharm-el-Shaikh, the statement said. Israel would not yield, as it had in 1957, to international pressure to withdraw from Sinai and the Gaza Strip, and to accept again that 'mixed bag of international arrangements and assurances' that collapsed a decade later.[11]

In February 1975, when rejecting the concept of a defence treaty with the United States, Prime Minister Rabin stressed this theme of self-reliance. Israel had always considered itself solely responsible for its own security in the Arab–Israeli conflict. He therefore pointed out that Israel did not want a defence treaty if this was supposed to be a substitute for Israel's minimum security demand – defensible borders. Moreover, while it wanted American assistance in obtaining weapons, Israel did not wish to lean upon America's readiness to send an army to its assistance.[12] Nor has Prime Minister Begin's public position concerning a possible American guarantee as part of a peace settlement been very different: 'We do not rely on any guarantees. We rely on our nation and on our army to prevent aggression'.[13] But there has been a noticeable shift on the subject of guarantees. Whilst the Israeli Government has continued to insist on an Israeli military presence in north-east Sinai and on the West Bank, Mr. Begin and his Ministers have also mentioned the possibility of a role for guarantors in the context of the Sinai.[14]

The Six Day War is said to have left Israel with an unprecedented degree of security requiring no external guarantees. It is true that the Suez Canal, the Golan Heights and the Jordan River provided Israel with borders which were both shorter and militarily easier to defend.[15] But even before the October War, whilst there was general public and private consensus on the need for secure borders as a pre-condition to any peace settlement, opinion was divided on the shape that these should take. Supporters of the Land of Israel movement, who believe in their biblical right to Greater Israel, opted for a maximalist map, whilst moderates, such as Allon, favoured conceding more territory for peace.

With the October War, a new strategic concept more in keeping with the views of the so-called 'doves', amongst them General Matti Peled, gained support in academic circles. Rejecting the occupation of territories, a new school opting only for minimal changes to the 1967 borders for security reasons, advocated the establishment of DMZs instead.[16] This is not to say that the concept of secure borders was lost to the strategic debate. The new school still wants secure borders, but believes that these might be obtained by taking political as well as military considerations into account, and by seeking any changes in the armistice lines considered necessary for minimum Israeli defence requirements, rather than by demanding maximum strategic depth on all fronts.[17]

The Allon Plan

First sketched out by Yigal Allon in 1967, this plan[18] represented, until the fall of the Labour Government in May 1977, the unofficial government position on border requirements. However, because this Plan still commands considerable support in Israel today, it should not be dismissd. It reflects a position between those advocating maximalist secure borders and the new school supporting withdrawal and demilitarisation: whilst based on military requirements, the Plan provides for substantial withdrawal and demilitarisation. Its purpose is to provide Israel with the 'essential minimum of security': minimal strategic depth, as well as lines which have topographical strategic significance.

Allon's formula would provide Israel with a defence posture which would enable its small standing army to hold back the invading Arab armies until most of the country's reserve citizens army could be mobilised. In addition to security zones along the Jordan River, on the Golan, in Sinai, and a land-route to Sharm-el-Shaikh which Israel would control to deter blockade attempts, there would be DMZs covering areas from which the Israeli Defence Forces (IDF) withdrew. Thus, Allon argues, Israel can compromise on territory and can concede 'all that is not absolutely essential to its security within the context of an over-all peace settlement'. But, he says, Israel cannot afford to compromise on security: 'The entire rationale of defensible borders is strategic'. Furthermore, using this rationale, Allon justifies 'selective settlement policy' in strategic zones as an integral part of Israel's defence system.[19]

But one factor, brought to light in 1977, throws doubt on Allon's minimal strategic argument, and the contention that his Plan would help solve the problem of the Palestinian identity. The so-called Allon Road (known as the 'limit of settlement road')[20] runs parallel to the Jordan River, but lies considerably to the west of the crest of the hills: at one point, it is as far as twenty-eight kilometres from the River. The Allon zone is not, therefore, a desert strip between the Jordan River and the eastern chain of the Samarian and Judaean mountains; it is a wide band of territory, which at Ramallah would reduce the width of the area for a future Palestinian entity to less than forty kilometres. Such an entity would comprise isolated Palestinian areas linked to the Arab world by a narrow and vulnerable corridor.[21]

Mr. Begin's Plan,[22] presented to President Sadat on Christmas Day 1977, represents the most recent Israeli position on borders. On the Sinai, it proposes a phased withdrawal of Israeli armed forces, demilitarisation of most of the peninsula, international guarantees to assure freedom of navigation in the Straits of Tiran

24

and a continued Israeli military presence to defend Sinai settlements. Terms for the West Bank and Gaza Strip are tougher: in short, the approximately 700,000 West Bank Palestinians would be granted limited autonomy, but they would have no sovereign rights; Israel would maintain a military presence for defence and public order. Although the Plan does leave the question of sovereignty to be decided, it implies that Israel has reserved for itself the right of veto over this critical issue.

Both the Allon and Begin Plans, as they stand, are totally unacceptable to the PLO and to Palestinians and Arabs generally.

Strategic Rationale of Defensible Borders

After the October War, there was considerable soul-searching amongst Israeli strategists. While those of the maximalist school said that the losses would have been more catastrophic on the old boundaries, some moderates belonging to the new school questioned whether the events would have happened at all had Israel withdrawn from occupied territories. The new defence burden in terms of expenditure and casualties since 1967 certainly did not reflect that greater security had been achieved by retaining territory, they argued.

So what is the strategic rationale for an Israeli presence of which Allon speaks? Whilst it is undeniable that Israel has legitimate security interests in occupied territories, some would argue that these are not best protected by even a limited Israeli presence.[23]

Sinai*

Israel's argument against an Egyptian presence in Sinai is well-known. Control of Sinai by a hostile party facilitates surprise attack on Israel: it permits forces to mass on Israel's borders, putting populated areas within vulnerable proximity. Before 1967, therefore, Israel considered (although this was not publicly stated) a major military build-up in eastern Sinai as a *casus belli*.[24] Not only might a major build-up presage an Arab offensive, but it could in itself economically strangle Israel. So, when President Nasser advanced his forces in May 1967, Israel had little choice but to launch a pre-emptive attack.[25]

* For a discussion of the Rafiah area, see Appendix I.

However, after 1967, with the Suez Canal as its new line of defence, Israel faced serious political and strategic problems. Israeli occupation of Sinai had so increased Egyptian political hostility that Egypt was now moved to take the offensive, both in the War of Attrition and in 1973. Not only did the Israeli objective of deterrence fail, but Israel was not prepared to use advantageously its presence on the Canal.[26] This was because the IDF preferred to fight with the desert behind it, rather than accept the political risk of a tactical sacrifice of territory that mobile fighting in the desert would have required.[27] But, while maintaining a rigid line of defence along the Canal might have been valid in terms of the strategic depth and early warning it gave, this strategy was not politically acceptable because of the long lines of communication and high death toll involved. The only advantages derived were: the distance of the fighting from populated Israel and the use of the air-base at Bir Gifgafa.[28]

Israel's concern with security is understandable. But in 1973, its military presence in Sinai created problems in military operations. In addition, this presence is unacceptable to the international community. Since Israel's problem has been to prevent a fatal concentration of Egyptian troops on its borders, and since both Egypt and Israel seek to benefit from the maximum warning possible, in terms of time and space, the principal requirement is for the widest band possible of effectively demilitarised territory. Then, large-scale violation would give evidence of hostile intent and time for counter-measures. The risks to Israel of withdrawal would thereby be reduced.[29] The question therefore arises: could an internationally-acceptable security system, based on effective demilitarisation of a wide band of territory in Sinai be devised? From Israel's viewpoint, it is, of course, the case that once the Egyptian capability to launch a surprise ground attack is neutralised, the Arab capability as a whole would be too.

Sharm-el-Shaikh

In the past, Israeli political leaders (including Allon) and military planners have argued that Israel must control Sharm-el-Shaikh to protect freedom of passage through the Straits of Tiran to the port of Eilat. Other senior Israeli officials, however, disagree. It is hardly convincing, they say, that control of the Sinai peninsula and a land-route to it are critical for Israeli defence. Why is this?

Those who demand control of Sharm-el-Shaikh compare the international support they are likely to receive in the event of blockades at Bab al-Mandeb and at Sharm-el-Shaikh. They claim that the international status of Bab al-Mandeb would prompt quick intervention by the Super Powers, as in 1973, when the Egyptians agreed to lift the blockade. But they point out that in the case of the 1967 blockade of the Straits of Tiran, international guarantees were useless – Egypt refused to lift the blockade. An Israeli presence at Sharm-el-Shaikh is required, they say, to serve as a trigger for military operations.

More significant perhaps is that an Israeli presence at Sharm-el-Shaikh and the 'crucial extra range this naval and air base provides, is a key to Israel's options'.[30] This means that if the Arabs blockaded Bab al-Mandeb or interfered with Israeli shipping destined for Eilat, Israel could retaliate by blocking both the Gulf of Aqaba and, more punitively, the Gulf of Suez to Arab and international shipping; alternatively, it could take air action against any Arab state bordering the Red Sea. Israeli strategists have maintained therefore that their bases at Sharm-el-Shaikh create a balance of blackmail.

By contrast, there are opponents to this scheme. The Begin Plan, overwhelmingly approved in Spring 1978 by the Knesset, drops the demand for sovereignty over Sharm-el-Shaikh, provided Israel's interests are protected there, and in the Gulfs of Aqaba and Suez, by some form of international guarantee of free passage by the major maritime nations. This shift in Israel's policy might well be based on the view held by Israeli Defence Minister General Weizmann that, once Sinai is demilitarised, Sharm-el-Shaikh would have little strategic significance for Israel.[31] It is argued that to prevent a blockade of Israel and to ensure freedom of navigation itself, Israel would need to control the shorelines of the Gulf of Aqaba from where the Jordanians or the Saudis could otherwise render the fifteen-mile-wide Gulf impassable. Moreover, Israel would have to control the Red Sea and the Bab al-Mandeb Straits. All these requirements would be totally impracticable.

Could not the threat of retaliatory action from Israel proper against international shipping passing through the Gulf of Suez deter a blockade of the Straits of Tiran as well as of Bab al-

Mandeb?[32] And if Israel's security lies not in its own control of the Straits, but in the prevention of blockade by another hostile power, an effective international presence at Sharm-el-Shaikh, providing a trigger for international support, could substitute for an Israeli presence.

The Golan

Until 1967, the advantages of the Golan Heights had allowed the Syrians sporadically to shell Israeli border villages in the Jordan and Hula Valleys during the disputes over DMZs; and northern Galilee, only 10–12 kilometres wide, lay totally exposed. The question of water supply was also hotly debated between Syrian and Israeli authorities.

After 1967, Syria's new positions no longer permitted its gunners to attack Israeli farming settlements directly. Territorial gains (particularly Mount Hermon) enabled Israel, with its sophisticated surveillance devices, to 'see' into Syria and Iraq, and the Golan Heights gave the IDF strategic depth of over thirty kilometres. This provided a strategic buffer beyond the international borders where the IDF could contain a Syrian advance whilst Israel mobilised. Those of the maximalist school who oppose returning territory on the Golan argue that if Syria had attacked in 1973 from its 1967 position on the Heights, northern Galilee would have been taken. Though they concede that Israeli villages are still vulnerable to attack from Syrian ground-to-ground missiles, this school argues that these alone cannot occupy territory. Israeli officialdom also maintains that whilst they do not dispute Syrian sovereignty, they are concerned with the security that the Golan brings: if the Syrians regained the Heights, they would hold a strategically-advantageous position; but with the IDF installed there, neither Israel nor Syria has a military advantage since both armies are within equal range of their respective vital areas.[33]

Is the Israeli territorial argument valid? The October War showed that it is still possible for Syrians from their more distant positions to shell villages in Galilee, and that Israeli observation on the Heights did not prevent a surprise attack. Moreover, Israeli critics of government policy say that the logic of Israel's argument for a strategic buffer has been undercut by the establishment of settlements, now twenty-seven in number, on the Heights. These settlements, together with the developments foreseen in the Five Year Plan, would need defending in a future war.[34] Logically speaking, therefore, another few kilometres should be taken to provide a cushion against attack.[35] In any case, in the event of attack, the exposed Golan settlements would complicate battle engagement and hamper reinforcements as evacuations took place. Thus, tactical and strategic advantages of the buffer apparently have been lost.[36]

As one Israeli academic has said: the geography of the Golan requires that the Syrians should not face Israeli troops on the Heights because the Israelis would constitute a direct threat on the plain leading to Damascus. Equally, Israelis in the Valley should not be threatened by Syrian troops on the Heights. This leaves open the question of who might sit on the Golan to ensure Syrian troops do not enter the area, and who might act as the necessary cushion should troops of either side choose to do so.[37]

The implication is that Israel's military presence on the Golan could be replaced by effective demilitarisation of the area without jeopardising Israel's security.[38] Furthermore, safeguards could be devised to give Israeli forces time to climb up to the Golan plateau so that a battle would not be fought on Israeli territory.

The West Bank

The pre-1967 lines posed a number of problems for Israel. Prior to the Six Day War, Arab medium artillery could reach almost all central Israel containing its chief centres of population and economic activity. Along Israel's narrow waistline, the distance between the Mediterranean and the Jordanian border ranged between nine and fifteen miles. Therefore, a surprise Jordanian armoured attack could have over-run central Israel, reaching the sea within an hour; but then a Jordanian army would, of course, find itself trapped by the IDF to the north and south.

There was also the terrorist threat. The populated Israeli–Jordanian border presented problems when it came to controlling raids. And the two bulges at Latrun and Tulkarm were seen as particularly threatening to the Israelis.

The former Labour Government argued that the security advantages of occupation were proved by the decline in terrorist raids from a peak of 111 in 1967 to 19 in the first ten months of 1973. But there was wide consensus that to preserve its Jewish and democratic character and to contribute towards a solution of the Palestinian issue, Israel should not annex an additional and significant Arab population.[39]

To solve the security and demographic problems, Allon therefore envisages only 'minor tactical border alterations' along the western section of 'the green line', but the retention of a strategic zone under absolute Israeli control along the Jordan River east of the dense Arab population. This would leave most of the Arab population of the West Bank under Arab rule (depending on the width of the strategic zone), but would give Israel the necessary strategic depth and topographical barriers to cope with a range of threats. It would enable Israel to pre-empt an attempt to cut its territory in two by surprise attack; to seal off the West Bank from East Jordan in order to prevent the introduction of heavy weapons or surface-to-air missiles (SAMs) in the West Bank; and to contribute to control of the area in the event of a re-initiation of guerrilla raids.[40] The last of these threats would be even more serious if Israel retained territory, as foreseen by the Begin Government, in the context of a settlement. Not only Rejectionists, but more moderate Palestinians, would resent and resist such an Israeli presence.

In the event of a threat of a surprise attack on Israel through the West Bank (which many outside observers consider unlikely), this could be dealt with by a régime of effective demilitarisation and establishment of early warning techniques once Israel had withdrawn. A token strip on the east side of the Jordan River might also be demilitarised to ensure that no outside force might suddenly be introduced into the West Bank. The more complex security problem would be the terrorist threat which Israel's policy of open borders between the West Bank and Israel would facilitate. The problem would be exacerbated further if Jewish settlers remained on the West Bank. It is arguable that the prevention of terrorism would be easier the greater the area handed back, because this would decrease scope for potential Palestinian grievance. Inevitably, withdrawal to 1967 borders would incur risks of armed incursions from both sides of the border, but partial withdrawal as envisaged by Allon could conceivably constitute the greater risk for Israel.

Security on the West Bank might therefore be best achieved if Israel handed back most of the region, together with the Gaza Strip, and if an international guarantor force, which would be more than an early warning force and at least as powerful and durable as an Israeli one, was established on the borders of the West Bank and Gaza Strip. Demilitarisation of evacuated territory, together with this additional guarantee, offers the best chance of a settlement that would satisfy Palestinian political demands without jeopardising Israel's national defence.

Lebanon

Israel does not expect to face the threat of a surprise conventional attack on its northern border with Lebanon; indeed, Israel does not regard Lebanon as a confrontation state. Nevertheless, since the Syrians intervened in Lebanon in 1976, the Israelis and Syrians have tacitly agreed that the thin Red Line (approximating the Litani River) should constitute the *de facto* security border between them. By contrast, there has been a continuing guerrilla threat to Israel's security from Lebanese territory. After 1965, when the Fatah organisation was founded, southern Lebanon provided a base for sporadic Palestinian fedayeen operations. Shelling across the Israeli–Lebanese border, infiltration and raids against northern Galilean villages escalated after the Six Day War, when the Syrians forbade Palestinian military activities across the Israeli–Syrian border. Then, when the Lebanese Government legitimised the Palestinian armed struggle in the form of the 1969 Cairo Agreement, and when King Hussein crushed the Palestinian commandos in Jordan in September 1970, southern Lebanon became the main military base for the Palestinian resistance.

The UN observers stationed on the Israeli–Lebanese borders since the 1949 armistice agreements had no mandate to cope with fedayeen operations.[41] So, Israel's answer to the growing guerrilla threat was to construct a sophisticated electronic detection fence, to conduct patrols on both sides of the border,[42] and to carry out reprisals in proportion to the Palestinian raids. But, in response to the Cairo Agreement, Israel intensified its retaliatory actions: limited border reprisals were substituted with surgical ground- and air-strikes against fedayeen training-camps

31

and logistical bases. Even when Palestinian commandos conducted operations from outside Arab territories, the Israelis responded against Lebanon, the only country where Palestinian military activities were not curtailed.[43] But in Lebanon, the objective of retaliatory policy (namely, to make the government responsible for restraining fedayeen activities) has not been achieved: Lebanese governments have been either unwilling or unable to control guerrilla operations in the south. For this reason, the former Israeli Labour Government considered that the only way to protect Israel's border villages would have been to establish an Israeli-controlled security belt in the Lebanon; but political constraints made this impossible.[44]

After November 1977, the PLO build-up in south Lebanon led to fighting between local Christians and the Palestinians and their leftist allies. This threatened the Israeli–Maronite Christian security arrangements along the border. Israel responded massively to this threat: first came the Israeli air-strikes in November 1977; then, in March 1978, after the PLO raid on the Tel Aviv road against a bus, Israel launched its long-planned incursion against Lebanon, occupying within three days an area up to the Litani River. The declared objectives were to establish a security belt and to eradicate the Palestinian commandos once and for all. Israeli officials insisted that Israel had no claim to Lebanese territory, but that they were concerned about the lack of Lebanese control over Palestinian military operations against Israel.

But was the Israeli massive intervention an appropriate response to the terrorist threat? After the Israeli incursion, the PLO commandos suffered casualties but were, in the main, merely driven north of the Litani River; from their new positions they could shell IDF forces in south Lebanon and Israeli villages, or launch sea-borne raids against Israel's coast-line. Moreover, Mr. Begin's critics argued that the logic of the military operation was undermined by the failure to take account of political considerations: Israel was unable to obtain a firm Syrian agreement to control the Palestinians north of the Litani. Also, the overwhelming military force used (which was intended to punish the PLO) killed hundreds of Muslims Shiites and Palestinian refugees: this indiscriminate action and new occupation of Arab territory further eroded international and American support for Israel.

In any case, the Israeli incursion exposed the fallacy of trying to

32

provide a military answer to the Palestinian political question. The PLO not only succeeded in its own aim of further stalling the peace process, but also proved that the Palestinians cannot be excluded from the Middle East equation: for the success of the UN peace-keeping mission in south Lebanon depends as much on PLO as on Israeli cooperation.

The international community had acted quickly to defuse the crisis by replacing Israeli military control with international forces. But the fact is that the ability of the UN force to restore order to the area and to provide Israel with the security it requires depends ultimately on progress towards a peace that includes a political solution to the Palestinian problem. Inevitably, after a peace settlement, the Israeli–Lebanese border would still be a focus for armed incursions by Palestinians rejecting a West Bank and Gaza entity; and should the Palestinians be offered less than this, then more-moderate Palestinians could be expected to join the Rejectionist resistance. Undoubtedly, Israel's policy of open borders would facilitate this potential terrorist threat. It follows, therefore, that the greater the area of the West Bank and Gaza Strip handed back to the Palestinians, the less serious might be the threat of guerrilla incursions across Israel's northern border, because the scope for Palestinian grievances would have been reduced.

So, security against a continued terrorist threat might eventually depend on a combination of meeting Palestinian minimum demands on the question of self-determination and of establishing an effectively-policed buffer in south Lebanon. In the absence of effective military control from Beirut, it may be that an international guarantor force with a mandate to cope with armed incursions would have to be established on this border. The United Nations Interim Force in Lebanon (UNIFIL) has already provided something of a precedent.

In the case of each border discussed, Israel clearly has a strategic interest, but it can be argued that this is not best protected by continued Israeli occupation. Indeed, Israeli occupation brought about the 1973 war, and in the absence of a settlement is liable to lead to yet another Arab–Israeli war – a factor to be taken into account in any Israeli strategic assessment. In short, it is not Israeli occupation *per se*, but the denial of occupied territories to hostile forces that matters, if Israel is to be protected.

Self-Reliance or Dependence?

There are other factors that cast doubt on the reality of the Israeli policy of self-reliance.[45] For as long as it refuses to give up territorial gains, Israel must depend on America, its single protector, for vast quantities of military and economic aid, as well as sophisticated weapons. A few indicators reflect the degree of this dependence: whilst it contributed 35.3 % of its 1976 GNP to defence,[46] Israel depended on America for approximately 32.2 % of its defence budget. In 1976, American public military and economic aid to Israel amounted to approximately \$2.4 billion and of this, approximately \$1,700 million took the form of military credits and grants.[47] Taken with the flow of money from the American Jewish diaspora, qualifying for American tax relief, the American contribution amounts to \$1,000 for every Israeli.[48]

Nor is it just the tangible military and economic aid that counts. Paradoxically, whilst Israel is the one country outside the industrial world able to produce the greatest variety of weaponry (meeting 30 % of its own defence needs) – thereby apparently diminishing dependence on the United States in certain weapon categories – this indigenous capability remains vulnerable to American influence. The net effect is that Israel's political dependence on America has grown.[49] Thus, a valuable export-earning industry has become susceptible, if only in part, to American political pressure – making Israel's fragile economy dependent on America too. With an inflation rate of 35 %, high tax rates, and a balance of trade deficit of more than \$3 billion in 1976, time is not on Israel's side.[50]

It cannot be taken for granted that American tax-payers will forever provide present rates of financial support. Indeed, Israeli policies have come increasingly to alienate the international community: it is felt by many states that it is now time to persuade Israel to act in conformity with UN resolutions, with the UN Charter and with declared American objectives.[51]

While the United States is and will remain committed to protect Israel's ultimate security, it cannot be expected either to continue to support Israeli occupation of Arab lands taken in 1967 or to acquiesce in Israeli operations such as the intervention in Lebanon in March 1978, thereby antagonising its chief foreign oil suppliers: in the first half of 1977, America imported 47 % of its oil needs of

34

which the Organisation of Petroleum Exporting Countries (OPEC) share was 84.4% and the Arab OPEC share 41.3%. The Middle East contribution is expected to increase further.[52] In addition, if American peace efforts should break down, there is the danger of recrimination and the radicalisation of the Arab world, with all the risks of a fifth war, threatening not only the cohesion of the Western alliance, but world peace. Also, with America's stake in the Arab world, and the effect this has had in eroding Soviet influence, Israel has become less valuable than before as a proxy. Though the diminution of Soviet influence could be a transient state of affairs, America will continue to be sensitive about maintaining good relations with the Arab world.[53]

Israel acts as an independent state and speaks as one. Nevertheless, with what some have seen as growing divergence between Israeli and American interests, the fact of Israeli dependence on America could create eventually an opportunity for peace by imposition.[54] Whilst the influence of America's Jewish 'lobby' should not be under-estimated, Washington's concern to protect its interests in the Arab world, which has led to its so-called 'Arab policy', has provided America, at least theoretically, with the potential to impose peace, which would logically lead to Israeli concessions. But if boundaries are settled in this way, the consequent loss of Israeli self-confidence and self-respect would entail a loss of psychological independence too. This could have destabilising and dangerous consequences.

Nuclear Option

Thus, the danger arises that, to rid itself of American diktat, Israel could choose the road to isolation by turning its nuclear potential into an open nuclear capability. This, it is argued, would be one way to avoid making unwelcome concessions.[55]

Nevertheless, Israel has pledged not to be the first to introduce nuclear weapons into the area: the political, economic and psychological costs would be high, and Israel would emerge as a latter-day Sparta.[56] Surrounded by a hostile sea of Arab states and with diminishing American support, Israel would become totally isolated from reality. Such an ultimate act of Israeli defiance could lead eventually to a break in American–Israeli relations, without which Israel could not survive. Moreover, there

35

is good reason to believe that the introduction of nuclear weapons by Israel, and the regional balance of terror that would inevitably follow, would be fraught with danger and would provide only limited deterrence.[57] In short, while it might provide Israel with a deterrent against a threat to its survival, it would bring little comfort or serve little purpose in the face of conventional attack or guerrilla incursions.[58]

Summary

Past military successes and scepticism about the value of external guarantees have encouraged Israel to define security in terms of defensible borders. This scepticism derives from unhappy experiences with the UN Emergency Force I (UNEF I) in 1967, and the failure of the world powers, particularly the United States, to take measures against the closure of the Straits of Tiran; but it also stems from the fear that guarantees are intended as a substitute for the security that Israeli control of present borders is thought to provide. Although Israel would inevitably require international guarantees on completion of a peace treaty, the very talk of guarantees before that point is reached is seen as a form of subtle pressure to force concessions that would not otherwise have been made.

It is frequently argued that due to demographic and economic factors, Israel can only buy temporary respite of, say, a decade by renewing hostilities. Most worrying to thoughtful Israelis is that the promise of *supply* of weapons alone might not be adequate to maintain Israel's military superiority for much longer. Although the economic balance between Israel and the Arabs has shifted radically since 1973, giving the Arabs the wherewithal to purchase more sophisticated arms, this potential has not yet been realised. Nevertheless, the change in the relative abilities of the two sides to command resources and the improvement in Arab fighting abilities have cast a shadow over Israel's long-term self-defence capability.[59] Israeli conventional military superiority cannot be counted upon indefinitely.

Moreover, political conditions – different to those prevailing when the Rogers Plan emerged in 1969, when the Israelis were enjoying air superiority over the west bank of Suez – now necessitate compromise. It is questionable, despite past declarations of support and the influence of the Jewish 'lobby', to what extent America can continue to support Israel against the United States' wider interests. There therefore seems to be a strong case for arguing that Israeli security may now be better served by an overall peace settlement involving territorial concessions, which would be underwritten by external guarantees, than by continued refusal to allow eventual self-determination for the Palestinians.

Neither the Begin Plan nor the so-called moderate Allon Plan for minimal defensible borders are formulas that either the confrontation states or the Palestinians would accept. The Egyptians demand every inch of their territory, the Syrians complete Israel withdrawal and the moderate Palestinians the right to self-determination on any territory relinquished by Israel. The PLO's spokesman on foreign affairs has confirmed that this means a Palestinian state on the West Bank and the Gaza Strip. Apart from possible minor rectifications, full withdrawal to 1967 borders is the Arabs' and Palestinians' minimum demand.

Nor is the extent of Israel's claim to defensible borders, whether in the form of the Allon or the Begin Plan, acceptable to the international community: there is no reason why Israel should expect its definition of secure borders to be accepted at the expense of the security needs and sovereignty of its neighbours. This would run counter to UN Resolution 242, which affirms the necessity for international security measures, namely DMZs, to protect the territorial inviolability and independence of all states in the area. Major modifications to the armistice lines would also be an infringement of the Preamble to UN Resolution 242, which specifies that it is inadmissible to acquire territory by force. In addition, for Israel to behave as if it is the only state in the area with a security problem at the expense of neighbouring states is contrary to the principle implicit in the UN Charter – namely, that a nation should not be permitted to expand its territories through conquest. There is, indeed, wide international consensus that there must be a full Israeli withdrawal with minor adjustments, and the establishment of a Palestinian entity on the West Bank and Gaza Strip.

Israel maintains an efficient army and will be self-reliant in the context of ability to provide itself with early warning and to conduct retaliatory raids if it chooses to pursue this policy. But it could not be self-reliant in a protracted war of attrition. If self-reliance – in the sense of a long-term war-waging capability – is no more than a myth, regardless of whether Israel perceives it as such; and if adherence to the Israeli interpretation of 'secure and recognized borders', which is premised on this myth, is likely to lead eventually to the introduction of nuclear weapons – the outlook is ominous.

The uniquely security-oriented definition of borders, together with the Allon and Begin Plans (despite their attempt to take account of the demographic factor) have been challenged in Israel and by prominent American Jews. For example, the Committee for an Israeli–Palestinian Peace prefers the return of territory, the creation of a Palestinian state and the notion of DMZs. It is its view that strategic and political considerations cannot be separated. This lends elasticity to the border issue. In exchange for a political settlement, an element of military risk is justified, say members of the Committee. Similarly, the Peace Now Movement, organised in March 1978 by a group of reserve officers and fast gathering momentum, calls for 'peace rather than territories'.[60] Rather than risk an imposed settlement and all the odium that would bring, or to pursue a dangerous isolationist path, both the Committee and the peace movement maintain that Israel should now retreat from untenable political positions.

Although the Begin Plan has been rejected by the PLO and Arab governments, it is on the crucial issue of the West Bank that compromise must be reached. Items to be negotiated include: the length of a transitional period before the issue of sovereignty is decided; the nature and placement of Israeli security forces and their police powers over the population in a transitional period; and the possibility of substituting international security arrangements for an Israeli military presence, at least after an interim period.[61]

The task, therefore, is to elaborate internationally-acceptable plans which would break the stalemate. On the one hand, the need is to provide Israel with the security and assurances it requires to withdraw (to 1967 borders with minor reciprocal rectifications). These should include Arab acceptance of an Israeli state.[62] On the other, such a security plan must also accommodate the Palestinian demand for self-determination and provide security for a future Palestinian entity, whatever its constitutional form, and for the existing Arab states.

Undoubtedly, flexibility must be shown on all sides; but the possibility of reconciling Israeli security needs and Palestinian and Arab political demands for the return of territory and Palestinian self-determination should not be ruled out. Mr. Begin has spoken in connection with the Sinai of international guarantees, anathema to previous Israeli Prime Ministers; and PLO leader Yassir Arafat has mentioned that he is prepared to accept an international emergency security force on the West Bank and Gaza Strip.[63] This is promising. It means that the local parties concerned have left open the issue of an international plan for security guarantees hinted at by President Carter in March 1977.

The time has therefore come for outside powers to consider in detail safeguards and guarantees as part of a comprehensive peace settlement. The linked issues of the Palestinian question and Israeli security could well become the major sticking-point in coming negotiations. But one way to persuade Mr. Begin to offer more to the Palestinians is to provide Israel with the strong external security guarantees it requires on its eastern front. It may well be that the promise of assurances in return for Israeli concessions is now the only way to avoid a fifth war.[64]

[1] The Israeli position on UN Resolution 242 is purposefully ambiguous. See *International Herald Tribune*, 24 April 1978. Early in 1978, Israel refused to acknowledge that the Resolution applied to the West Bank and Gaza Strip, although it agreed that it required withdrawals in Sinai and on the Golan. But by April, in a Cabinet communiqué, Israel firmly accepted UN Resolution 242 as a basis for negotiations with all its neighbours: Egypt, Lebanon, Syria and Jordan, and that Mr. Begin's Peace Plan was compatible with it. *Jerusalem Post International Edition*, 28 March 1978; *The Daily Telegraph* (London), 17 April 1978.

[2] In October 1976, the British Government spoke of a 'home' for the Palestinians. But it was in March 1977 that President Carter first used the term 'Palestinian homeland'. This concept was later endorsed in the Declaration of the Nine of June 1977.

[3] See Appendix for a map of the 1949 borders.

[4] Mr. Begin's Plan presented to Egypt in December 1977 is an elaboration of his Plan of July 1977. For part of the text of the Plan, see *The Times* (London), 29 December 1977.

[5] Note that the twelfth session of the Palestine National Council in June 1974 adopted a ten-point transitional political programme, which stated that in the event of an Israeli withdrawal from the West Bank and Gaza Strip, the PLO would accept the establishment of a national authority in these parts of Palestine.

[6] *United States Information Service (USIS)*, 10 March 1977.

[7] Speech to the Knesset. See *The New York Times*, 13 June 1967.

[8] Yair Evron, *The Middle East: Nations, Super-Powers and Wars*, Elek Books Ltd., London, 1973, pp. 83–85.

[9] Ambassador Gunnar V. Jarring of Sweden, UN special representative, undertook a new peace initiative in the Middle East in February 1971. He submitted identical letters to the governments of Israel and Egypt, soliciting replies on a series of questions.

[10] *The Times* (London), 13 March 1971.

[11] *New Middle East*, No. 31, April 1971.

[12] *Brief*, No. 100, 16–28 February 1975. Also interview data.

[13] Interview with Israeli television, 4 July 1977, Summary of World Broadcasts, 6 July 1977.

[14] It is worth noting a recent remark by Dayan on this subject which leaves open the possibility of a positive Israeli response to an American guarantee offer. According to *The Daily Telegraph* (London), 2 September 1977, Dayan has said that the Israeli Government had no knowledge of 'a serious American readiness to guarantee Israel's security with American forces in an operational manner, as part of a peace settlement'. See also *Jerusalem Post International Edition*, 20 September 1977.

[15] However, Israeli occupation of the Sinai meant that long coastlines had to be defended.

[16] Despite references made by Israeli decision-makers to demilitarisation, detailed discussion remains confined almost entirely to the circles of academic strategic analysts. See Dan Horowitz, 'Israel's Concept of Defensible Borders', *Jerusalem Papers on Peace Problems*, No. 16, 1975, p. 23, n. 83. The Committee for an Israeli–Palestinian Peace in Israel also supports this approach.

[17] Ibid., pp. 20, 29.

[18] See Appendix for a map of the Allon Plan. Yigal Allon, 'Israel: The Case for Defensible Borders', *Foreign Affairs*, October 1976, pp. 38–53.

[19] Ibid.

[20] See Appendix for a map of the Allon Road.

[21] Elizabeth Monroe, '"Allon Road" puts doubt on Carter's "Homeland"', *Events*, No. 15, 22 April 1977, p. 26.

[22] This is a re-formulation of the Begin Plan of July 1977, which resembled Dayan's Plan for a 'functional' division of power over the West Bank and Gaza Strip with Jordan.

[23] See, generally, Colonel Merrill A. McPeak, 'Israel: Borders and Security', *Foreign Affairs*, April 1976. Also Allon, op cit., p. 41.

[24] Yair Evron, 'The Demilitarisation of Sinai', *Jerusalem Papers on Peace Problems*, No. 11, February 1975, p. 6.

[25] Alternatively, Israel might have invited UNEF I to cross the border.

[26] Total control of Sinai has always been rejected by senior Israeli officials. Note that both Foreign Minister Dayan and Prime Minister Begin have said that full control of Sinai is not an Israeli objective.

[27] Despite its preference for mobile warfare, Israel fought with the desert at its back – the rationale being that the Super Powers might stop the fighting before Israel had recovered territories sacrificed for tactical reasons. See Horowitz, op. cit., p. 21.

[28] The Bir Gifgafa air-base is important because it provides Israel with an air operations capability that would give Egypt minimal early warning. Israeli anxiety to keep the base is illustrated by the shape of the buffer zone lines drawn in the 1975 Sinai Interim Agreement.

[29] These questions were all raised in the Egyptian–Israeli Military Committee established at the Sadat–Begin Ismailia Summit.

[30] Mordechai Abir, 'Sharm-al-Shaikh/Bab al-Mandeb: The Strategic Balance and Israel's Southern Approaches', *Jerusalem Papers on Peace Problems*, No. 5, March 1974, p. 26.

[31] General Weizmann is on record as saying that to maintain that Sharm-el-Shaikh and the Straits of Tiran are necessary for Israel's survival is 'ridiculous'. See Eric Rouleau, 'Les Entretiens Carter–Begin: Les Atouts d'Israel', *Le Monde*, 19 July 1977. See also *Financial Times* (London), 27 August 1977.

[32] If, however, the Israeli Government's argument is that an Israeli base at Sharm-el-Shaikh increases its options for offensive military operations – facilitating control over Suez, the Gulf and the Red Sea – this is another matter. But again, the kind of peace negotiated with the Arabs, and accompanying safeguards and external guarantees, could justify the return of Sharm-el-Shaikh.

[33] Background Paper, 'Golan Heights', 1974, *Carta Jerusalem*; see also Allon, op cit., p. 48, for a similar view.

[34] In a statement delivered in the Knesset on the Separation of Forces Agreement with Syria, 30 May 1974, the then-Prime Minister, Mrs. Golda Meir, said of the Agreement: 'We have taken care to safeguard the military line as well as the security of all our settlements on the Golan Heights and their continued strengthening, consolidation and development'. *Information Briefing*, No. 25, Israel Information Centre, Jerusalem.

[35] Dayan himself has hinted at some disadvantages as well as advantages: on the one hand, the front is further away from populated Galilee; on the other, any withdrawal in battle would cause severe damage to the settlements on the Heights. See Moshe Dayan, *Story of My Life*, Weidenfeld and Nicolson, 1976, p. 383.

[36] For an interesting discussion, see Meir Merhav, 'Defence Wall or Barrier to Peace', *Jerusalem Post International Edition*, 26 September 1977.

[37] Michael Brecher, *The Four Questions: A Dialogue in Cairo*, unpublished, June 1975.

[38] McPeak, op. cit., p. 432.

[39] According to a recent projection assuming a continuing high Arab birth-rate, a decreasing Jewish birth-rate, zero net immigration, the Arabs in the present *de facto* borders would constitute an absolute majority of 51.6 % by the year 2000. See D. Friedlander and C. Goldscheider, 'Peace and the Demographic Future of Israel', *The Journal of Conflict Resolution*, Vol. XVIII, No. 3, September 1974, pp. 486–501.

[40] For a discussion of the security issue of the West Bank, see McPeak, op. cit., pp. 432–434; Allon, op. cit., p. 47; Horowitz., op. cit., pp. 26–27.

[41] See Michael Comay, 'U.N. Peace-Keeping in the Israel–Arab Conflict, 1948–75: An Israel Critique', *Jerusalem Papers on Peace Problems*, No. 17–18, 1976, p. 61.

[42] Edward Luttwak and Dan Horowitz, *The Israeli Army*, Allen Lane, 1975, p. 312.

[43] For example, in December 1968, Israel destroyed 13 'planes of the Middle

East Airlines at Beirut International Airport. This was in retaliation for an attack by two Arabs on an El Al 'plane at Athens Airport, involving one death.

(44) Luttwak and Horowitz, op. cit., p. 312.

(45) The concept of self-reliance in military matters implies that a border that is not defensible in the military sense is not secure. Horowitz, op. cit., p. 5, f. 1.

(46) *The Military Balance 1977–78*, IISS, London, 1977, p. 83.

(47) Fiscal year June 1975–June 1976, plus the transitional phase, July–October 1976.

(48) Eric Rouleau, 'Les Entretiens Carter–Begin: Les Atouts d'Israel', *Le Monde*, 19 July 1977.

(49) For example, the export of certain Israeli manufactured weapons, such as the Kfir jet, require an American go-ahead because they contain American components. In early 1977, the United States vetoed export of Kfirs to Ecuador.

(50) George W. Ball, 'How to Save Israel in Spite of Herself', *Foreign Affairs*, March 1977, p. 464.

(51) The Rogers Plan of 1969 and the Brookings Institution Report are two such guides. Also, in November 1975, Deputy Assistant Secretary of State for Near Eastern and South Asian Affairs, Harold Saunders, testified before a Congressional sub-committee: 'In many ways the Palestinian dimension of the Arab–Israeli conflict is the heart of the conflict ...'. By 1976, the Saunders statement was taken to represent a new American approach to the Palestinian problem.

(52) In 1973, the OPEC share of total American oil imports was 70.2 % and the Arab OPEC share 22 %. See *The Daily Telegraph* (London), 14 September 1977, which quotes figures from the Federal Energy Administration of the US Government as reported in the *Oil and Gas Journal*.

(53) Carter's package arms deal supplying 'planes to Israel, Egypt and Saudi Arabia, ratified by Congress in May 1978, was a reflection that the shift of American interests in the Middle East has been widely recognised in the United States. Though the package does not alter the balance of military power against Israel, it does indicate that America will be thinking about its future arms policy with relation to the Middle East. This Israel must take into account.

(54) For an interesting discussion, see Mark A. Bruzonsky and Israel Singer, 'Dependent Israel: The Two Options', *Worldview*, April 1976.

(55) See Robert W. Tucker, 'Israel and the United States: From Dependency to Nuclear Weapons', *Commentary*, November 1975.

(56) See Allon's re-affirmation of this pledge, *Jerusalem Post International Edition*, 14 September 1976. Nevertheless, former Chief of Staff Mordechai Gur has said that Israel would keep up with any development of Arab nuclear weapons. *Jerusalem Post International Edition*, 16 November 1976.

(57) Yair Evron, 'A Nuclear Balance of Deterrence in the Middle East', *New Outlook*, Vol. 18, No. 5, July–August 1975. There is also the argument that should both Israelis and Arabs acquire an open nuclear weapon capability, then the balance would swing marginally in favour of the Arabs. Israel's very existence would be at stake as opposed to the survival of a number of Arab cities on which Israeli weapons would be targeted.

(58) A more detailed discussion of the nuclear aspect of Israeli defence policy is outside the scope of this paper.

(59) See Richard H. Ullman, 'After Rabat: Middle East Risks and American

Roles', *Foreign Affairs*, January 1975, p. 290.

[60] The peace movement, which criticises Begin's settlements' policy and his insistence on indefinite military occupation of the entire West Bank, has won the public support of prominent American Jews and Israeli academics. See *The Guardian* (London), 3 April 1978; *The Guardian* (London), 25 April 1978; *International Herald Tribune*, 25 April 1978.

[61] See Robert Stephens, 'Big Breakthrough – or a False Dawn?', *The Observer* (London), 1 January 1978. However, the Plan perpetuates the Israeli demand for territory and retains an Israeli veto on the issue of sovereignty.

[62] This would not exclude the possibility of Palestinians pursuing by peaceful means PLO leader Yassir Arafat's original dream of a democratic secular state in Palestine. Faruq Kaddoumi, the PLO spokesman on foreign affairs, said in an informal briefing in London in October 1977 that in return for a 'mini-state', the Palestinians would renounce their armed struggle and would work to recover their rights in the rest of Palestine by non-violent means. *The Times* (London), 3 October 1977.

[63] The force, he said, should be made up of troops from the five permanent members of the UN Security Council. Reported by *Al Ahram* (Cairo) and broadcast by the BBC World Service, 8 January 1978.

[64] Chapters 6 and 7 will examine how safeguards and guarantees might be effectively implemented on each front.

3. ROLE OF THE SUPER POWERS I:

THE AMERICAN APPROACH TO GUARANTEES

Incompatibility between Israeli and Arab demands makes it unlikely that the local parties will reach a peace settlement themselves. For while the Israelis demand limited withdrawal and a full peace, the Arabs want complete Israeli withdrawal, a limited peace[1] and Palestinian self-determination. Could third parties, therefore, help bridge the gap between these irreconcilable positions? Could they guarantee the sovereign states of the area within agreed borders during the long process of normalisation of relations?

There can be no absolute iron-clad guarantee. But while UN peace-keeping forces, DMZs and formal guarantees cannot ensure absolute security, reliance on one's own power alone cannot, in the long run, ensure this either. It may therefore be to everyone's long-term benefit to accept the best guarantees presently available.[2] What might these be?

The purpose of safeguards (early warning devices) and guarantees (promises to take action in support of a threatened state) in the Middle East would be to protect the frontiers and territorial inviolability of all states in the area, including a Palestinian 'homeland' (whatever its political status), from a range of possible threats. It would be naïve to suggest that after years of bitter struggle, a political settlement in itself would produce neighbourly relations and stability. Incidents would be bound to occur and the challenge is to find a security system which would make fighting almost impossible. This would require separating the protagonists where possible, thereby reducing their opportunities to use weapons against each other or to invade by way of surprise attack or infiltration.[3] On Israel's borders with the West Bank and Gaza Strip (and possibly with Lebanon too), where there could be no meaningful separation of forces and where the security problem becomes more acute, an international guarantor force capable of preventing terrorist incidents and reprisal raids would be required. Without doubt, security measures devised to protect all borders would be enhanced by carefully applied arms limitations that would help reduce the likelihood of surprise attack.

However, a security system that seeks to protect borders and to limit arms must also assure the local parties that its arrangements would be respected. The Brookings Report has foreseen the possibility of an 'eventual limitation of the flow of arms into the area' as part of the security arrangements, and the potential need for 'supplementary' guarantees by the Great Powers. But here the Report ends inconclusively: 'The Congress might well, however, consider favourably some form of guarantee of a comprehensive peace. ... If at any time it should appear that a supplementary unilateral guarantee to Israel alone or to other parties as well were essential to the conclusion of a settlement, we believe such a guarantee would be in the U.S. interest. It seems probable that a guarantee to all of the parties should best be multilateral, extended by the Soviet Union and perhaps Britain and France as well as the United States'.[4] If, then, safeguards such as DMZs and UN forces are considered insufficient to prevent violations of the agreements – and this would be the Israeli objection, particularly with regard to the West Bank – it would be precisely the nature and credibility of the Great Power guarantees that would determine the acceptability of the security package. This would apply not only to Israel and its friends in America, but also to Arab states and Palestinians who have their own security needs. Who should provide such guarantees and how would it be done?

An essential question is whether the American Administration can or will apply the necessary pressure on Israel to withdraw to its approximate 1967 borders. To do this, the Administration must devise a credible and effective security system to forestall accusations that America has sacrificed Israel.

President Carter's Middle East diplomacy has stimulated discussion of the safeguards and external guarantees of a security package: DMZs, international peace-keeping forces, electronic early warning stations, multilateral and/or unilateral guarantees. But the American Administration has so far not stated precisely what role it would play as guarantor. Washington has always been cautious about extending a formal unilateral guarantee to Israel. And it cannot impose and maintain a complex security system on its own.

Historical Perspective

The two forms of unilateral American guarantee most often talked about have been:
  i) a formal defence treaty with Israel, supplementary to local party and international security arrangements; and,
  ii) an American guarantee of borders agreed by the two sides.

The idea that the existing *de facto* alliance between Israel and the United States should be formalised in a defence treaty is not new.[5] On the few occasions that the Administration has spoken of a possible treaty, it has always done so cautiously. On 26 August 1955, Secretary of State Dulles offered a formal treaty 'to prevent or thwart any effort by either side to alter by force the (agreed) boundaries', but he added the proviso that he hoped 'other countries would be willing to join in such a security guarantee, and that it would be sponsored by the United Nations'. Moreover, a negotiated agreement on boundaries was to precede treaty arrangements.[6]

During the 1960s, America sought to maintain regional stability through a balance of power in the area and treated Israel as a military proxy. It became a significant arms supplier under the Kennedy and Johnson Administrations, and in 1962 President Kennedy assured Israel's Foreign Minister, Mrs. Meir, that America and Israel were *de facto* allies.[7] However, Israel never received the more formal American commitment that Prime Minister Ben Gurion had sought during the 1950s.

After 1967, Washington increasingly appeared to look on Israel as a tacit ally in the context of Super Power rivalry, while Israel, with extended borders, but (because of General de Gaulle's veto) being deprived of French arms, became more dependent on the United States. American commitment to Israel became a means of balancing the Soviet presence in the area as well as an instrument of persuasion in the search for peace. On 23 July 1970, to induce Israel to accept the Rogers cease-fire plan, President Nixon privately offered a formal political alignment if a peace treaty was

46

agreed.[8] His offer fore-shadowed Senator Fulbright's proposal on 26 August for a mutual defence treaty to supplement a peace imposed and guaranteed by the United Nations, on condition that Israel withdrew to the 1967 borders.[9] This was seen by many as a possible final extension of the *de facto* relationship.

In the aftermath of the October War, the American long-term commitment to Israel was re-affirmed in the framework of the American 'Arab policy'. Fearful of the oil weapon being used again, the United States pursued a policy of military and diplomatic support to Israel based on the condition that Israel should help to bring about a peace settlement. The guarantee idea re-emerged, but this time emphasis was placed on compensation for Israeli withdrawal. In November 1973, while in Peking, Secretary of State Kissinger publicly indicated that a mutual security treaty was a possible way of guaranteeing Israel's future boundaries,[10] but with the usual proviso that discussion of the form of guarantees should come only after peace negotiations. However, by the beginning of 1975, he is reported to have ordered a study of guarantees of Israel's independence and security in return for a withdrawal to 1967 borders.[11]

Amongst American commentators, the focus on guarantees and particularly the treaty idea had become more intense as the full implications of a further crisis for Super Power relations and for oil supplies dawned. Some considered that only a treaty obligation would be strong enough to persuade Israel to concede territory. For them, the concept of a guarantee became central rather than supplementary to a settlement.[12] A mutual defence treaty was seen as an 'imperative necessity' to be entered into after a peace treaty.[13] It was said that with the possibility of a fifth war, the United States should force a settlement and sign a military pact.[14] Moreover, it was proposed that a bilateral treaty between the United States and Israel, whereby the former would bind itself to send American forces to help the latter, would be the key element in a future guarantee framework.[15]

Other commentators went further, suggesting that an American military presence in Israel should play a deterrent role. This was because the promise of American supplies was considered no longer sufficient for Israel's security, given the changed economic and military balance in the area. In place of an ambiguous commitment to Israel's survival, or a treaty, which would not necessarily bind future Administrations, Ullman called for 'an overt and explicit commitment' to Israel's defence. Unlike past promises, he said, this would be a 'military alliance' with a US guarantee 'made visible by the presence of US forces', as in West Germany. But for the commitment to become effective, the Israelis would have to withdraw approximately to their 1967 boundaries. The guarantee would 'substitute for the normalisation of relations' and give the Israelis the confidence required to withdraw 'without requiring their enemies to reach a formal agreement with them'. *De facto* peace would be sufficient and the American guarantee would replace one form of security with another.[16]

Step-by-step diplomacy both reflected and encouraged this new focus on guarantees as a *sine qua non*. Kissinger frequently suggested that the scope of military commitments to Israel would be determined by Israel's readiness to rise above narrow military advantages in the interest of political ends.[17] Under the January 1974 First Disengagement Agreement, Israel received substantial promises from America in a secret Memorandum of Understanding. But the culmination of step-by-step lay in the 1975 Sinai Interim Agreement: in its draft form, the American–Israeli Memorandum of Agreement is said to have amounted to a formal political and military alliance between Israel and the United States.[18] Even in its final form, it contained a substantial open-ended commitment: the United States promised to be 'fully responsive within the limits of its resources and Congressional authorization and appropriation, on an on-going long-term basis to Israel's military equipment and other defence requirements, to its energy requirements and to its economic needs'; re-affirmed its long-standing commitment to the survival and security of Israel and pledged to consult with Israel if its security was threatened by a 'world power'; assigned two hundred civilian personnel to early warning stations in Sinai; and promised to conclude within two months a contingency plan for supplying Israel militarily in an emergency.

For the Israelis, the American presence demonstrated the depth of the American commitment to stability in the area and was seen as a deterrent. According to the then-Defence Minister Shimon Peres, it was 'tantamount to virtual American involvement' in Israel's security.[19] Even American officials saw it as a fore-runner of an American security treaty in the context of a peace settlement.[20] But to allay the fears of Congressmen, Kissinger confirmed at the Sinai Hearings in October 1975 that the documents were generally statements of intent except for the legally-binding clause concerning the provision of oil.[21] In substance, the Agreement represented a codification of the existing American–Israeli relationship and Kissinger maintained that it did not go significantly further than past American commitments to and understandings with Israel.[22]

A Unilateral American Guarantee of Borders and of Demilitarisation

A distinction should be made between a guarantee in the form of a defence treaty with Israel and a guarantee of its borders. These are quite different propositions. On the one hand, a defence treaty would represent a formal commitment to come to Israel's aid if its survival was at stake – a commitment extended informally by President Truman and every President since his time. On the other hand, because this is a strategically and geographically constricted area and because of the psychological fears on both sides, a guarantee of borders would ideally require a guarantee to keep certain areas demilitarised. Broad bands of demilitarisation, approximately corresponding to those areas from which the IDF withdrew, together with token demilitarised areas of Israeli territory, would be intended to make surprise attack and infiltration virtually impossible, thereby providing all-important psychological reassurance to both sides. Clearly, in operational terms, the maintenance of demilitarisation in Sinai and on the Golan would differ from that on the West Bank and in the Gaza Strip. A unilateral guarantee of borders, therefore, would necessarily involve the United States in a commitment to support a régime of demilitarisation – meaning ultimately to compel a violator to retract after an infringement had taken place or, in the case of the West Bank, to prevent a violation from occurring in the first place. Such a unilateral guarantee is unlikely to be acceptable to the American Congress.

The 1975 Sinai Interim Agreement marked a departure from previous American reluctance to accept unilateral responsibilities. The United States had undertaken a 'limited' but 'crucial' responsibility, said Dr. Kissinger.[23] If not a 'guarantor', the

United States was 'involved', said Under Secretary of State Sisco.[24] Apart from the monitoring activities of the American civilians to verify compliance with the Agreement, their presence constituted a form of symbolic deterrent. Hesitant about taking on commitments risking military involvement abroad, and in no mood to undertake a treaty commitment which would heighten the risk of future military involvement, Congress studied the Agreement closely and inserted escape clauses into the Joint Resolution: American personnel would be withdrawn if hostilities broke out, or if replacements could be found. And Kissinger alleviated fears by confirming that sending two hundred technicians to Sinai was not comparable to early steps taken in Vietnam, and by reassuring Senator Clark that nothing in any American commitment under the Agreements involved the use of armed forces.[25]

With the Sinai Field Mission (SFM) providing a degree of tactical early warning, the question of further use of American personnel under future agreements has become a talking point. As early as 1975, the idea was suggested by an American official.[26] By Summer 1976, Senators and their staffs speculated about the feasibility of extending the limited American role to other fronts in a peace settlement.[27] Admittedly, said a senior American diplomat on the spot, the restricted geographical areas and population of the Syrian and Jordanian fronts would complicate matters. Moreover, the 'hostage' aspect would be stronger because American civilians would be more vulnerable to attack by terrorists.[28]

Obviously, a future Sinai-type monitoring role on other borders would have to fit in with American priorities. Clearly Washington would wish only to perform such a role if the settlement in all of its parts was acceptable to Arab oil producers and if the Soviet Union did not choose to use the American presence as an excuse for an obstructionist role. Furthermore, both Congress and American public opinion would need to be convinced that such involvement was in the American interest. For the Israelis, it would be the visible demonstration of American involvement and its deterrent effect that would count.

Not surprisingly, therefore, State Department officials have said that any future use of American personnel in the Middle East would have to be both 'limited' and 'temporary', and that each case would be 'closely scrutinised'.[29] The reasons are starkly clear. A limited symbolic commitment in support of effective demilitarisation is one matter. Anything more extensive and permanent, such as the deployment of American forces intended as a 'trip-wire', is another.

Even if Congress acquiesced, such a presence in DMZs would be a limited deterrent rather than a guarantee: for instance, under what circumstances should the American forces take action? Would the United States be equally willing to act against both local parties? (As in the case of the 1950 Tripartite Declaration, the result of an 'impartial posture' might well lead to the use of force against neither.) Then there would be the question of whether the American soldiers alone should take action in the event of a limited occupation of a DMZ; and how they should act against terrorism or Israeli retaliatory raids across DMZs, if international forces and other safeguards failed to prevent these occurring. Moreover, a unilateral physical presence might provoke the Soviets to seek advantages where possible. For example, in a calculated bid to gain influence, the Soviets might support a limited Arab violation, provided this did not risk a Super Power confrontation. The suggestion that Congress is likely to agree that an American civilian presence should be accompanied in a final settlement by an American military presence to help guarantee DMZs does not therefore seem possible.[30]

A Possible Soviet Spoiler's Role

There are other drawbacks. To argue that an American unilateral guarantee of the separation of forces on all fronts could be written into an agreement; or, less ambitiously, that American civilian personnel could be sent to all fronts, would be to assume that the local powers, whatever their future shape or political colour, would not insist on including the Soviet Union. Whereas we had been told in the foreign policy circles of America and Europe that the Arabs would not want the Soviets to participate in guarantees, we found the position to be quite different. Egyptian, Jordanian, Syrian and PLO leaders alike all insisted that they would wish the Soviet Union to share the responsibilities of a settlement and of their security. This is because they consider that Soviet

51

participation would guarantee that America would continue to be firm with Israel.[31]

Moreover, both Super Powers talk of the need to limit arms transfers to the Middle East in the event of a settlement. And if a suppliers' agreement (see Chapter 6) limiting arms transfers is to succeed, the Soviet Union, as a major supplier, must be party to it. If not, it could easily prevent a durable peace. Free of guarantee obligations, the Soviet Union would wait in the wings. The prospect of instability brought about by a coup d'état, inter-communal conflict, or social unrest would always be there – facilitating opportunities for Soviet penetration of the area as in the past. Radical régimes and movements woud probably want contacts with the Soviet Union – an important source of arms and technical aid. Nor would the Soviet Union readily refuse support to friendly Arab states or a Palestinian 'homeland', if asked, partly for fear that the prestigious role of arms supplier might be lost in part to China.

In the unlikely event of the Soviet Union agreeing to restrict arms supplies without demanding participation in guarantees of other agreements, and if the local parties concurred in its exclusion, one can imagine the Rejection Front, with the political encouragement of the Soviets, using 'salami tactics' – small violations of DMZs, etc. – to make political gains.[32] So, while the Soviet Union cannot impose its will on the Middle East, it does have 'considerable capacity for obstructing a general settlement', as the Brookings Report says. This view was privately endorsed in Arab capitals and amongst Palestinians who agreed that the involvement of the Soviet Union in the negotiating process and guarantees of a settlement was a necessity.[33]

Then there is the other argument which commands more support: if the Soviet Union agreed to abandon its role as a supplier of arms, its chief source of influence in the area, it could be expected to make substantial political demands in return. At the very least, it would wish to extend its status as a Power with Middle East interests. This would probably mean playing an equal role with the United States in guaranteeing the settlement in all or most of its parts. It appears that the Soviets, who have expressed displeasure at step-by-step diplomacy, would be unwilling to acquiesce in any extension to other areas of the current American role in Sinai, or in a unilateral American guarantee of DMZs.

Soviet participation in guarantees of DMZs and of frontiers would be likely to become a *quid pro quo* for their agreement on arms limitations.[34]

The United States, therefore, is unlikely to want formally to guarantee the separation of forces by itself. Nor would the Soviet Union's wish for political parity permit this. The United States thus faces a dilemma. To bring the Soviets into the process earlier rather than later, and to include them as an equal in safeguards and guarantees, means forfeiting benefits (however short-term) reaped through unilateral diplomacy. On the other hand, as some American observers and Egyptian officials have pointed out, to pursue unilateral diplomacy longer than necessary or to exclude the Soviet Union from safeguards and guarantees is likely to encourage a Soviet spoiler's role – thereby jeopardising peace negotiations and the feasibility of credible security arrangements.[35] The United States has to be sensitive to Soviet interests and to its demands, as Co-Chairman of Geneva, to play a greater role in peace-making, as well as to its concern for political parity.

Thus, if the above analysis is correct, guarantees of borders and of DMZs should be multilateral. Partially for domestic reasons and partially because of the Soviet factor, Secretary Dulles in 1955 and Secretary Rogers in 1972 preferred the multilateral option. The Brookings Report also draws attention to it.[36] The Four Powers could extend such guarantees (the form of which is discussed in Chapter 4) to all of the parties.

An American Defence Treaty with Israel

Despite the urgency with which some American academics viewed the concept of a formal defence treaty after 1973, the examples cited show that official thinking on the subject has been consistently circumspect. Not wanting to undertake formal commitments in politically unstable circumstances, the US Administration has only offered a formal alignment to Israel on completion of a peace treaty.

Nevertheless, the idea of a formal unilateral American guarantee for Israel has not been abandoned. Congress reportedly would approve one, but only after detailed scrutiny of commitments involved once a comprehensive peace had been achieved.[37]

It also appears that the Administration might, at least, be contemplating the offer of a formal alignment in return for an Israeli evacuation of territories occupied in 1967. What form this could take is an open question. In his election campaign, President Carter referred to the possibility of a unilateral defence treaty,[38] and since then, the State Department has at least toyed with the idea of a unilateral guarantee and, less convincingly, of a possible naval base in Israel.[39]

Israel publicly maintains that it neither asks for, nor wants, such a formal link, possibly because this might undermine its negotiating position with the Arabs, be taken as a substitute for defensible borders, and limit its present freedom in taking the initiative (as it did in 1967). However, privately, informed Israeli sources concede that because it would be legally binding, a mutual defence pact might be welcome, but only after a settlement.[40] Furthermore, tangible evidence of a reversal in Israel's previous negative attitude towards external guarantees came with its acceptance of American technicians in Sinai.[41]

Past American arguments against an offer of a formal alliance with Israel are well-known:

i) It would be disadvantageous for America to link itself to Israel in unstable circumstances prior to withdrawal to approximate 1967 borders.

ii) It would be disadvantageous to tie itself formally to Israel in any circumstances because of the present uncertain phase of détente with the Soviet Union: by boxing itself into a rigid relationship with Israel, America would be inviting the Soviets to offer similar assurance to the Arab states and perhaps to a new Palestinian entity. If those states entertained such an idea (and this is open to question), Super Power military rivalry could be dangerously formalised in a chronically unstable area (but see p. 57 for another view). And if current favourable American–Arab relations were to deteriorate, the Arab–Soviet relationship would be encouraged, possibly at the expense of America's 'Arab policy'. In a crisis, the United States might then find itself uncomfortably on one side of a partition line between American and Soviet spheres of influence, with vital oil supplies on the other. This could jeopardise American relations with NATO allies and Japan.

iii) America would not welcome the increased Israeli leverage over itself that an alliance would bring: as a formal client state,

Israel could involve its protector by activating certain treaty provisions. Whilst America's lack of enthusiasm for a formalised Soviet presence in the Middle East is predictable and its commitment to Israel's survival deeply held, Washington would not wish to let Egypt or Syria become a Russian proxy to be contained in the same way as the Soviet Union. Indeed, it is likely to regard the development of relations with Egypt as an alternative and possibly safer way of reducing Soviet influence in the area. Dulles was unwilling to extend a treaty to Israel in 1957 in exchange for military bases because of the danger of being drawn into confrontation which would jeopardise links with the Arab world.[42] Likewise, in a peace context, America will want to enjoy good relations with Arab states. A formal American guarantee of Israel explicitly *against* Egypt or Syria would not be acceptable.[43]

iv) To be credible, a treaty guarantee would have to specify what steps would be taken to meet specific contingencies, including the required use of force. No such explicit commitments have been offered in the past. And it is unlikely that Washington would offer them in the future. The Eisenhower Declaration of 20 February 1957 endorsed a secret aide mémoire sent from Dulles to Ben Gurion. This committed the United States to exercise the right of free and innocent passage in the Gulf of Aqaba. But, after the closure of the Straits of Tiran, Washington would not act alone, and could not get collective support to enforce free navigation. With the United States deeply involved in Vietnam and fearful that American interests in the Arab world would be hurt, Congress opposed American intervention, and was even uneasy about a collective Allied initiative. Because of the strong Congressional feeling, President Johnson sought to reinforce Eisenhower's Middle East Resolution with a new one authorising the use of force. Before he was able to do so, war broke out. In short, the reliability of a treaty guarantee would be more likely to flow from the physical presence of the Americans in the area.

If a comprehensive peace settlement had been reached and its confirmation came to depend on whether America would or would not offer Israel a defence treaty, the advantages of doing so would seem to outweigh the disadvantages outlined above. In any case, some of these would not apply after Israelis and Arabs had approved and signed a peace treaty. With a stake in the peace, the likelihood of war would have been reduced. As for other reservations, the very form of the guarantee and the provisos attached could take account of these.

The function of a formal alliance as far as Israel is concerned would be to act as an ultimate deterrent against any future Arab régimes which might reject Israel; to provide Israel with the long-term confidence needed to withdraw from the occupied Arab territories; to provide an added insurance for Israel if arms limitation measures (such as those described in Chapter 6) failed to function; and, most importantly, as a guarantee against Soviet intervention. In other words, to provide a guarantee of 'last resort' of Israel's security.

In brief, in order to meet these needs, Israel would want an explicit assurance that the United States would not only continue to provide military and economic aid necessary to its security, but that it would also be ready to act in specified contingencies, and by the use of force if necessary, to guarantee Israel's ultimate security.

Such an alliance could also be an advantage to the Palestinians and other Arabs. Although a formal American guarantee of Israel's security might appear too one-sided in what was meant to be a balanced package of safeguards and external guarantees, it would be scarcely more significant than America's constantly re-iterated *de facto* alliance with Israel.[44] Apparently it would not incur the odium of the present régimes in Egypt and Jordan, for Sadat is on record as saying he would not oppose an American–Israeli defence treaty as part of a Middle East settlement; and according to a member of the Jordanian Royal Diwan, Jordan would not object either.[45]

If necessary, the United States might consider a similar guarantee to neighbouring Arab states for their ultimate security. This might put America in as embarrassing a situation as it already occupies over Cyprus in relation to Greece and Turkey, or, conversely, it might have a restraining influence: one ally (Israel) would hesitate before attacking the other ally (Egypt) of its own ally (the United States), and *vice versa*. It is possible that if America was asked to give a defence treaty to Israel as a guarantee of 'last resort',the Palestinians might then consider the security measures set out in this study as insufficient for their own security. The possibility of a Palestinian–Soviet alliance (however embarrassing for the Soviets) could not be excluded – an eventuality that would be unacceptable to Israel, America and the moderate

Arabs, and that would upset the possibility of 'neutralising' a new Palestinian entity. Alternatively, both Super Powers might together either offer a joint guarantee of 'last resort' to the new Palestinian entity, or agree to abstain from doing so (thereby treating that entity as non-aligned) provided the Palestinians agreed.[46] But if the Palestinians were to insist that they had the right as much as Israel to choose who should be their own guarantor of 'last resort', then Israel might decide that this was too great a cost to pay for a defence treaty with the United States, and drop its request on condition that the Palestinians opted for non-alignment.

Just as an American–Israeli alliance would serve as a deterrent against an Arab attack, it could be expected to restrain Israel from an over-hasty pre-emptive attack. It would also bring America increased leverage over Israel by restraining it from provocations and reprisal raids. Israel would not willingly challenge those safeguards with which its ally, America, might be visibly identified (see Chapter 5).[47]

For their part, the Americans would not want to undertake a guarantee that was more extensive than necessary: least controversial might be a provision for naval facilities and a mutual defence pact, or a mutual defence pact on its own.[48] A mutual defence pact would be likely to take the form of that with Korea or Japan. The former requires each party to 'meet the common danger in accordance with its constitutional processes', whilst the latter obligates the United States to defend Japan. Provisos attached to any mutual defence pact would ideally be:

i) that it accompany a comprehensive settlement endorsed by the UN Security Council;

ii) that it be undertaken only to supplement multilateral guarantees of the borders of Israel and its neighbouring states;[49] UN forces in DMZs and other practical safeguards in which the Soviet Union, together with the United States, would be physically involved; guarantor forces with a special mandate on the West Bank and Gaza Strip and on the Israeli–Lebanese border;

iii) that it would obligate the United States to deal, by use of force if necessary, only with violations which could not be dealt with by other guarantee arrangements;

iv) that it would not obligate the United States to come to the

57

assistance of Israel if Israel was the party which chose to go to war, or was responsible for initial major violations of the settlement (unless Israel's survival was subsequently threatened);

v) that it would be restricted to major violations threatening the ultimate security of Israel or world peace.

[1] President Sadat's position has been ambiguous in the past. In April 1977, he spoke of full normalisation with Israel within five years and dropped the view that there could only be peace in the next generation. *International Herald Tribune*, 11 April 1977. But, in July, it was reported that he had said Egypt would accept the existence of Israel as a Middle East state if it conformed to the demands of international legality. *Financial Times* (London), 21 July 1977. However, Sadat's visit to Jerusalem is now taken to represent Egyptian recognition of Israel as a state.

[2] Fred J. Khouri, *United Nations Peace Efforts* in Malcolm H. Kerr (Ed.), *The Elusive Peace in the Middle East*, State University of New York Press, Albany, 1975, p. 93.

[3] For an interesting discussion on the preceding points, see Ian M. F. Smart, 'Military Insecurity and the Arab–Israel Conflict: There is an effective alternative to the United Nations', *New Middle East*, No. 26, November 1970; see also Fuad Jabber, 'Not by War Alone: Curbing the Arab–Israeli Arms Race', *The Link*, Vol. 7, No. 5, November/December 1974.

[4] The Brookings Institution, *Toward Peace in the Middle East*, Washington, December 1975, pp. 14, 22–23.

[5] For a full discussion on the feasibility and credibility of an American unilateral guarantee for Israel, see Michla Pomerance, 'American Guarantees to Israel and the Law of American Foreign Relations', *Jerusalem Papers on Peace Problems*, No. 9, 1974.

[6] Cited in Mark A. Bruzonsky, 'American Thinking about a Security Guarantee for Israel', *International Problems*, Autumn 1976. Note that the Kennedy Administration, which in 1963 linked a solution of the refugee problem to American guarantees, was also only prepared to countenance security guarantees in the context of a peace settlement.

[7] A written assurance sent from President Kennedy to Prime Minister Eshkol the following year contained a virtual guarantee of Israel's territorial integrity. See Michael Brecher, *Decisions in Israel's Foreign Policy*, New Haven, Yale University Press, 1975, p. 322.

[8] Lawrence L. Whetten, *The Canal War: Four-Power Conflict in the Middle East*, The MIT Press, 1974, p. 116.

[9] On several occasions since 1970, Senator Fulbright renewed his call for a formal treaty obligation to Israel – in May 1973 in the Senate, at the Pacem in Terris Conference of October 1973 and after his tour of the Middle East in 1975. See N. A. Pelcovits, 'Security Guarantees in a Middle East Settlement', Foreign Policy Research Institute, *Sage Publications*, 1976, p. 4.

[10] *International Herald Tribune*, 13 November 1973.

[11] James Reston, 'A U.S. Guarantee for Israel', *International Herald Tribune*, 22 February 1975.

[12] For an interesting discussion of the concept of an American guarantee, see Mark A. Bruzonsky, *A United States Guarantee for Israel?*, The Centre for Strategic and International Studies, April 1976.

[13] Nadav Safran, 'The War and the Future of the Arab–Israeli Conflict', *Foreign Affairs*, January 1974, p. 215; and 'Middle East: The Fleeting Opportunity', *The Nation*, 5 April 1971, p. 425.

[14] William E. Griffith, 'It's Our Move in the Middle East', *Reader's Digest*, February 1975, p. 72.

[15] Charles W. Yost, 'Mideast: Is it Peace or War Ahead?', *Christian Science Monitor*, 7 August 1975.

[16] Richard H. Ullman, 'After Rabat: Middle East Risks and American Roles', *Foreign Affairs*, January 1975, p. 295; see also Ullman, 'Alliance with Israel?', *Foreign Policy*, Summer 1975, pp. 27, 30, 31. Similar suggestions have come from others.

[17] Edward R. F. Sheehan, 'Step by Step in the Middle East', *Foreign Policy*, Spring 1976, p. 37.

[18] Ibid., p. 60.

[19] *U.S. News and World Report*, 8 September 1975.

[20] *International Herald Tribune*, 28 August 1975.

[21] *Early Warning System in Sinai*, Hearings before the Committee on Foreign Relations, United States Senate, Washington, 1975, p. 223.

[22] Ibid., p. 237.

[23] Ibid., p. 208.

[24] Cited in Pelcovits, op. cit., p. 29.

[25] Sinai Hearings, op. cit., pp. 218, 240. The issues raised in Congress and the caution shown reflected the post-Vietnam tide of public opinion. A number of polls during 1975 showed that Americans did not favour commitments that risked troop involvement. And a *National Observer* readership plebiscite taken in mid-September 1975 indicated 77 % opposed to the assignment of American technicians to Sinai. Pelcovits (op. cit., pp. 28, 62, n. 57) cites the Harris Survey of Spring 1975 and the Gallup Poll of Summer 1975, which found 12 % in favour of sending troops to save Israel, and a *Time*-sponsored survey which found one-third against sending troops to Israel in case of aggression.

[26] See Marilyn Berger, 'U.S. Precedent Seen in Pact', *The Washington Post*, 4 September 1975.

[27] Interview data.

[28] Interview data.

[29] See Wolf Blitzer, 'Americans in the no-man's-land', *Jerusalem Post International Edition*, 8 February 1977.

[30] The suggestion is put by Yair Evron in 'The Role of Arms Control in the Middle East', *Adelphi Paper*, No. 138, IISS, London, Autumn 1977, p. 32.

[31] Interview data. For a Jordanian point of view, see Renée Short, 'Jordan: ready for the prize of Middle East peace', *The Times* (London), 17 May 1978. See also Yassir Arafat's interview with *The New York Times* reported in the *International Herald Tribune*, 3 May 1978.

[32] Some sceptics argue that the Soviet Union might want to avoid the risk of being part of any guarantee of demilitarisation, preferring to let the Americans

entangle themselves in this particular responsibility.

[33] Interview data.

[34] The limits of Soviet tolerance have been expressed to the authors on a number of occasions in their talks with Soviet and Middle East officials.

[35] Interview data.

[36] In January 1972, in response to a question about 'the prospect of the U.S. actually offering a guarantee of any borders the two sides agree on', Rogers said, 'I don't think that the U.S. individually as a nation would undertake that. I think that the U.S. will consider possibilities of some kind of U.N. guarantee'. *Department of State Bulletin*, 24 January 1972, p. 91. Cited in Mark A. Bruzonsky, 'American Thinking about a Security Guarantee for Israel', *International Problems*, Autumn 1976, p. 79.

[37] *The Sunday Times* (London), 10 July 1977. See also Brookings Institution, op. cit., pp. 22–23.

[38] *Le Monde*, 20 October 1976.

[39] Eric Rouleau, 'Une Étape Décisive pour le Proche Orient: La Confrontation Carter–Begin', *Le Monde*, 8 July 1977. *Financial Times* (London), 6 July 1977. See also *International Herald Tribune*, 23 September 1977. US officials have discussed the feasibility of a US naval base in the area. But they insist that a naval base in Israel would only be considered as part of a final settlement and if it was clear that it would not upset the Arabs.

[40] Israelis are aware of the limitations of a formal treaty: treaties can be abrogated and the 1973 War Powers Act limits Presidential commitment of troops abroad without Congressional authority to 60 days. But, although the effectiveness of a commitment is less related to its form than to the guarantor's perception of its national interest, Israelis note the 1969 National Commitments Resolution which states that only obligations expressed in treaty form are legally binding. They also attach importance to the psychological value of an American–Israeli treaty as a supplement to other security measures. As for a possible US naval base, in September 1977, Foreign Minister Dayan told Congressmen that he would be pleased to allow America to establish a base at Haifa for use by the Sixth Fleet. Israel would cooperate, he said, to demonstrate its dependability as an American ally in the region. *International Herald Tribune*, 23 September 1977.

[41] For former Defence Minister Shimon Peres' attitude to American monitoring stations, see Sheehan, op. cit., p. 61.

[42] The Tripartite (US, Britain and France) Declaration proved an empty promise because the guarantors preferred not to risk jeopardising relations with Egypt by supplying arms to Israel to counter the 1955 Soviet arms deal with Egypt. But in fact the French had already supplied arms to Israel prior to the Soviet arms deal with the Egyptians.

[43] The Brookings Institution (op. cit., p. 23) considered that one criterion of external guarantees should be that they underwrite a settlement and not be directed against anyone. See also Alan Dowty, 'The Application of International Guarantees to the Egypt–Israel Conflict', *Journal of Conflict Resolution*, Vol. XVI, No. 2, June 1972, p. 260.

[44] *The Guardian* (London) of 3 October 1977 has quoted a statement by Dr. Zbigniew Brzezinski broadcast in an American television interview as follows: 'If Israel was mortally threatened, especially by an external power, the US, even now, without a security treaty, would certainly go to its aid'.

[45] *International Herald Tribune*, 8 July 1977. Also interview data.

[46] Yassir Arafat has said in an interview with *The New York Times* that 'the only possible solution' to the Middle East problem is for the United States and the Soviet Union to provide guarantees for Israel and a Palestinian state. *International Herald Tribune*, 3 May 1978.

[47] There is the question of whether a pre-emptive strike by Israel, in the face of an anticipated massive Arab attack, would nullify an American guarantee of last resort. Another major obstacle in future guarantee arrangements will be the Israeli doctrine of retaliation against violations by irregular forces operating from one of the Arab states whose borders are likely to be guaranteed multilaterally. By its restraining effect, an alliance could supplement any early warning devices or guarantor forces designed to prevent incursions from both sides of an Israeli–Palestinian border (see Chapter 5).

[48] The presence of a naval base at Ashdod or Haifa would seem unnecessarily provocative. Congressional insistence that base agreements should take treaty form reflects recognition that an American presence is as binding, if not more, than a written treaty. For an interesting discussion of a US treaty guarantee, see James Reston, 'Offering Israelis Solid Guarantees', *International Herald Tribune*, 10 April 1978.

[49] Much thinking on Capitol Hill and amongst American academics envisages multilateral guarantees of a settlement, and favours the inclusion of other NATO members. Their views agree fundamentally with the findings of the Foreign Policy Decisions Programme poll that a multilateral guarantee would be twice as preferable as a unilateral guarantee in return for Israel's withdrawal from occupied territories and acceptance of an independent Palestinian state. See Great Decisions 1976 Opinion Ballots, 20 April 1976. Also interview data.

4. ROLE OF THE SUPER POWERS II:

I) POSSIBILITY OF JOINT AMERICAN SOVIET GUARANTEES

The Soviet Union as a Co-Guarantor

In 1973, when the Soviet Union became Co-Chairman of the Geneva Peace Conference, it was in effect recognised as a Power with legitimate Middle East interests. The United States may hold nearly all the negotiating cards, but its special relationship with Israel precludes it from having the sort of dealings that the Soviet Union has with the PLO. And the fact is that the Arabs' capacity to hold Israel to a draw has been due to the Soviet Union providing the Arab states with arms and other forms of support. The potential for obstructionist tactics deriving from these Soviet links and from its role as arms supplier makes the Soviet Union a necessary partner both to the peace-making process and in arms limitation agreements. Soviet cooperation in maintaining a military balance at a lower level by agreeing to regulate the flow of arms will be as essential to the preservation of any settlement as is Soviet diplomatic cooperation at Geneva, or any other peace conference centre, in bringing it about.

If the Israelis are to be persuaded to withdraw, they are likely to call for some sort of American presence in buffer zones, as they did in 1975. In which case, given Soviet demands for political parity, the price of Soviet support for the settlement and for arms control arrangements is likely to be an equal presence, whatever its form. It then becomes counter-productive for the United States to try to include the Soviet Union in one form of guarantee or safeguard but not in another. Super Power guarantees of a military balance and of DMZs are implicitly linked. They are not the 'icing on the cake', as Kissinger described them, but ingredients essential to the success of a settlement.

In 1976, some senior State Department officials, who were close to Kissinger, were cautious about allowing the Soviets anything more than a political guarantor role. They objected that an 'institutionalised presence' of any sort would give the Russians an advantage they do not have at present. Recognition of Soviet parity with the United States in the Middle East was and probably still is considered an unnecessary concession.[1] There is a powerful argument against this viewpoint: namely, that Russian participation in guarantees is both desirable and necessary to keep the area steady. For, besides the enormous disadvantages of excluding the Soviet Union from guarantees, there are advantages in its involvement.

By sharing responsibility as political co-guarantor of the peace settlement with the United States (and others), it is true that the Soviet Union would gain the prestige it seeks. But participation on the ground as backers of DMZs is likely to further raise the Soviet stake in peace.[2] Visible identification with the successful maintenance of DMZs is likely to encourage meticulous observation of linked arms control arrangements by the Soviet Union. Whatever the form of their physical presence (to be discussed), the personnel of both Super Powers would become 'hostages', which would have a restraining effect on the local parties. These latter would not easily challenge international forces supported on the spot, no matter how, by their own ultimate backers. In brief, the danger of a Soviet 'wrecking role' would be reduced and the Americans would not have to pay the unknowable political cost of attempting to extend a unilateral guarantee of DMZs.

Some sceptics argue that with a Russian presence on the ground, even if only that of staff officers or civilians, the risks of Super Power confrontation would be greater. Against this supposition, it can be said that with a settlement accepted by all sides, the risk of war would have been reduced. In any case, as the past has shown, small incidents, even involving Super Power personnel casualties, do not necessarily lead to Super Power reaction, let alone confrontation.[3] Moreover, if the Super Powers are involved in upholding the peace, any violation of the new frontiers would automatically involve them. By playing a watch-dog role on the spot, both Russians and Americans would see any build-up and could resort to mediation or pressure before aggression took place. If they sought to defuse crises in this way, the likelihood of Super Power confrontation would diminish. In general terms, a practical role of this sort would provide an opportunity for the Soviet Union to engage in détente.

Finally, the presence of the Super Powers should have an effect on the vitally important question of the durability of the arrangement. It should reduce the likelihood of one of them withdrawing its visible backing of the settlement. For it is unimaginable that, once committed, either Super Power would wish to leave the other as the sole Super Power presence.

Soviet Concern for Peace in the Middle East

If both Super Powers are to be present in DMZs, the question arises whether they want peace in the Middle East and can cooperate to maintain it, despite the choices and possible sacrifices involved.[4]

In Summer 1976, some senior State Department officials questioned whether the Soviets either wanted or had anything to gain from backing peace.[5] This approach is based on the belief that the Soviets favour instability, provided that this does not risk Super Power confrontation; it assumes a potential Soviet 'spoiler's role' in both negotiating and post-settlement processes. Those who believe this conclude that the United States could best limit Soviet influence by offering the least opportunities for Soviet participation in a settlement. However, for the reason given above, this strategy could, in fact, offer the Soviets the greatest opportunities for making trouble.

This school also argues that if the Soviet Union preferred a peace settlement to the present instability, it would have pressed the Rejection Front to show moderation and persuaded Yassir Arafat to find a formula that would satisfy the State Department, if not Israel, that the PLO was prepared to offer Israel *de facto* recognition. There is, in fact, some evidence that the Russians have made an effort in this direction.[6] However, Soviet leverage can be over-stated and attempted persuasion could be counter-productive. Egyptian observers and a number of Soviet academics have warned that if the Palestinians were over-pressurised into accepting less than the West Bank state demanded by their moderates, then, sooner or later, the Rejectionists would increase their following.[7] Willingness to persuade the Palestinians to compromise over their minimum demands may not be the way to achieve stability in the future and the Russians might not be willing to guarantee a settlement of this obviously unstable nature.

Another approach, and this is not without support amongst some Israeli government advisers, says that the Russians now consider détente with the United States so important that they would prefer stability in the Middle East, provided they could play an equal role in bringing it about. Supporters of this view say Soviet concern for peace is illustrated by the way they have pursued their interests in the past. It is undoubtedly true that since the mid-1950s, the Middle East conflict has been a unique asset, providing the Soviet Union with opportunities to influence the Arab states. On the one hand, it has been concerned to gain support facilities for its naval force in the Mediterranean; while on the other, it has wanted to deny the region to American hegemony. Another Soviet interest lies in acquiring status and prestige. Since the 1950s, Moscow has invested a good deal in terms of aid, military hardware and reputation to become a Middle East Power. Today, it would like to confirm the political parity that was achieved when the Soviet Union became Co-Chairman at Geneva.

Even at the zenith of its influence in the area, the Soviet Union's behaviour always showed a consistent pattern of restraint. The Soviets confined themselves to the supply of certain types of arms to Egypt, Syria, Iraq, North and South Yemen and to diplomatic declarations of support for their clients. There was no sign of a readiness to risk war on behalf of these clients; in fact, formal commitments in the region were studiously avoided.[8] The Soviets have only indicated an intention to intervene under specific circumstances: to counter American support of Israel or to safeguard the vital interests of a client. Thus, in 1967 and 1973, they threatened to intervene to defend Damascus and in 1973 to save the Egyptian Third Army, and they directly involved their pilots, aircraft and missile crews in the last six months of the War of Attrition when Israel started deep-penetration bombing of Egypt.

These threats were not required under any Soviet commitment, but were judged necessary to safeguard the Soviet political position in the area and to prevent any loss of prestige from abandoning clients in the face of catastrophe. For example, the failure to re-supply the Arabs after the Six Day War would have entrenched feelings of disillusionment caused by the lack of concrete Soviet support during that war. Thus, the sale of arms, originally intended for political reasons, and the establishment of military facilities had brought about a *de facto* Soviet commitment as firm as any formal arrangement might have been.[9]

But the *de facto* commitment was nevertheless limited. The Soviet Union showed restraint in terms of the arms supplied and in the way fighters and SAMs were deployed.[10] There is little doubt that Moscow recognises the dangers of an American–Soviet confrontation inherent in the Arab–Israeli conflict and that support for Arabs under certain circumstances is incompatible with détente. Undoubtedly, the October War tested détente, and some say that the Soviet Union violated détente agreements by its behaviour at that time.[11] Kissinger judged that an act of confrontation had occurred and that the détente relationship had not prevented it, but that this relationship had made it possible to defuse a dangerous state of affairs.[12]

Similar caution is reflected in Soviet relations with the PLO, to whom they have never openly afforded more than verbal encouragment.[13] Although the PLO and Yassir Arafat, as its leader, enjoy Soviet political support, the Russians are unwilling to damage their international image by openly endorsing terrorist tactics. However, their influence over the PLO should not be over-estimated. In consistently saying that the parties directly involved should decide on the form of PLO representation at Geneva, the Soviets have tacitly admitted they do not have an effective say in the matter. Similarly, on a Palestinian state, the Soviets are on record as saying that territory for consideration would be the West Bank and Gaza Strip. What is uncertain is how influential the Russians would be in persuading the PLO to make the necessary concessions if proposals for guaranteeing such a state were forthcoming. In broad outline, the Soviet Union's commitment to the PLO is moral and ideological, rather than material.[14] It recognises the PLO as 'the legitimate representative of the Palestinian people' and accepts the necessity of PLO participation at Geneva. Whether the Soviets would support more extreme PLO demands is open to considerable doubt. They have, however, left enough flexibility in their degree of commitment to allow them to take a revised Palestinian position if they should later wish to do so.[15]

Soviet policy has thus steered a difficult path between arming the weaker party and restraint to avoid world war risks. Until 1972, the Soviet Union was prepared, in the interest of regional stability, to accept unpopularity with the Arabs by applying restraint in its dealings with Egypt – and to a lesser extent with Syria – by denying them the war option. It may well have been the heavy price in unpopularity it had paid in preventing the Arabs from going to war that encouraged the Soviet Union in early 1973 to adopt a higher risk policy by stepping up deliveries that included some key offensive weapons, such as the Scud surface-to-surface missiles (SSMs), to act as a counter-deterrent to Israel's Phantoms.[16]

Admittedly, if the Soviet Union chose to commit itself to peace and guarantee a settlement, which it has publicly offered to do, it might involve renouncing opportunities to gain prestige by supplying arms. China would not only resort to accusations of 'socialist imperialism', but might well become 'the spoiler'. Nevertheless, Soviet academics say that a settlement, and the stability this would bring, would be preferable to the risks of a further Arab–Israeli war. Western diplomats in Moscow believe that if the Americans can persuade the Israelis to withdraw, the Russians would be unlikely to undermine a settlement, because their fear of military risks is too great.[17] The Soviets would not, however, be willing to pay an unreasonable political price. It is generally agreed that they would want to play an equal role, not only at Geneva, but in maintaining a settlement. In any case, a political and practical co-guarantor role would bring the Soviets the international prestige they seek. Moreover, if the military option was excluded, at least between Arabs and Israelis, Super Power political rivalry would be relegated to the safer field of ideological and economic competition.

Political Feasibility of Super Power Cooperation

That the Super Powers can cooperate in the Middle East in the interests of peace has been demonstrated in the past. Forms of cooperation have varied and a distinction must be made between tacit and actual cooperation.

Stated briefly, examples of cooperation are:
i) unilateral self-restraint in supplying arms by one Super Power

designed to influence the pattern of arms transferred by the other (as when America delayed Phantom deliveries to Israel in 1971 and Russia refused jet fighter-bombers and SSMs to Egypt in 1970–72);[18]

ii) *de facto* cooperation over inspection of the 1970 cease-fire with each of the Super Powers relying on its own independent surveillance techniques. As one commentator noted at the time, 'Out of this could come a habit, a beginning of mutual confidence, and an acknowledgement of mutual interest upon which could be built more elaborate collaboration in other forms'.[19] On that occasion, the cease-fire broke down, but the precedent was promising. Since then, American aerial surveillance has become a central element of verification under the 1975 Sinai Interim Agreement and the Soviets are assumed to carry out their own satellite and Mig-25 reconnaissance;[20]

iii) diplomatic cooperation, of which the 1969 Two Power Talks, the joint drafting of UN Resolution 338, and the joint American–Soviet statement of 1 October 1977 on the principles and objectives to govern a re-convened Geneva Conference are examples.[21]

Clearly, cooperation has been possible when it has been in the self-interest of both Super Powers. This has meant that either the political cost has been low (as in the case of the 1972 Joint Statement of Principles Governing Relations between the Soviet Union and the United States) or the danger of non-cooperation leading to Super Power confrontation has been high. By contrast, of course, cooperation has been severely circumscribed or undermined when the Super Powers have perceived their self-interests differently. Then one of them has pursued unilateral advantage, and even engaged in brinkmanship, to win political prestige in the eyes of its clients.[22] Détente may have helped to settle the 1973 crisis: but should détente policies be left unsupported by practical commitments to maintaining peace, Super Power rivalry would probably revive and accelerate.

However, practical cooperation also presents difficulties. A mere joint political endorsement of a settlement in the form of a declaration of intention would not achieve much. But, given the degree of rivalry, more active cooperation poses problems. Were

68

the Super Powers to undertake joint policing, they would have to agree on who had violated the peace and what action to take. Inevitably, interpretations would differ. And if positive decisions and actions had to be taken, this would require an effective command structure. Even supposing the role of commander were to alternate betwen the two Powers, or was somehow shared by American and Russian officers acting together, the result must be unpredictable and dangerously confusing. As Israeli and American diplomats pointed out, either Super Power could exercise a paralysing veto.[23] Or, if permitted under the agreement, one of them could intervene unilaterally.[24] Thus, a 'joint' guarantee that involved action by the Super Powers might be used to legitimise unilateral Soviet intervention.[25] The fear expressed is that such a guarantee might not only fail to operate and lose its credibility, but the scope for Super Power crises might increase.

As for the participation of Super Power military contingents in an international force, which is consistently advocated by the French,[26] obvious difficulties would arise relating to cooperation and command. Neither Super Power could accept the command of the other; nor is it imaginable that they would readily agree to subordinating their contingents to, say, a Finnish commander. Quick action and mobility in the face of violation would be effectively ruled out. In addition, there would be the problem of stationing Super Power combat troops. To avoid identification of one Super Power with any one country and to prevent polarisation should incidents occur, combat troops of both Super Powers would have to work together in each DMZ. Would Israel agree to Soviet troops on its soil?

According to French experts, one way round this conundrum of command would be for a force including contingents of the Four Powers (and China, if it agreed) to act merely as a static deterrent force or 'trip-wire'. It would (i) include contingents from the Four Powers and, for political reasons, from the Third World; (ii) be a static and lightly-armed force along the frontiers with no active role; (iii) need no orders from the Security Council and the Force Commander would have the limited mandate of maintaining a presence and a right to resort to force in self-defence; (iv) require the assenting vote of the Security Council to be removed.

The formula has merit because it recognises (i) the practical difficulties of the Super Powers playing an active role; (ii) the importance of a Super Power presence on the ground which would fulfil a 'trip-wire' function – thereby acting as a deterrent; (iii) that a system based on a static UN presence and on moral or political deterrence would reduce the need for recourse to the Security Council, minimise the confrontation risk, and be more acceptable to contributing states. It should be noted, however, that both the United States and the Soviet Union have reservations about participating in a Middle East peace-keeping force (see pp. 72–78). And, although the Israelis and Soviets would certainly resume diplomatic relations with a peace settlement, Israel (and Egypt as well) would prefer the Soviets in a non-combatant role on its borders.

At present, the Super Powers cooperate mostly by agreeing not to do certain things, rather than by acting together. Examples of such passive or negative cooperation are the Antarctica Treaty (1959), the Partial Test Ban Treaty (1963), the Nuclear Non-Proliferation Treaty (1968), the agreement on biological weapons control (1972) and the first SALT agreement of 1972. Similarly, the Super Powers have successfully agreed not to disturb the potentially volatile situation of Berlin. Both have also been careful not to infringe the different kinds of neutrality of two virtually undefended countries lying between their military spheres: Austria and Finland. How, then, might the Super Powers engage in a similar form of limited cooperation in the Middle East context?

II) THE FORMS OF SUPER POWER COOPERATION

UN Security Council Resolution

To be workable, a security system that depends on effective safeguards, guarantees and arms control needs the backing and cooperation of both Super Powers. The question is, what form should their cooperation take to avoid the difficulties sketched above?

The Super Powers could cooperate under the aegis of the Security Council, but there would be limits to the role that the

United Nations could play in the context of a settlement. The international framework for the peace would be a resolution of the Security Council to endorse the settlement and to establish peace-keeping machinery.[27] In this way, the Soviet Union would be fully committed and the interest that France and Great Britain have in participating would be accommodated. The resolution would most certainly be drafted under the terms of Chapter VI (Pacific Settlement of Disputes) of the UN Charter. Under this Chapter, endorsement would avoid the possibility of impracticable enforcement if any of the parties failed to comply, while ensuring that the UN peace-keeping force should not be removed without a positive resolution of the Security Council. It seems that insufficient political will exists amongst UN member states to build on the Congo experience and to create a further precedent for the use of force other than in self-defence.

Formal Multilateral Guarantees

But a verbal commitment of this sort by the Super Powers endorsing the settlement and backing peace-keeping machinery would not be sufficient guarantee for the local parties, particularly Israel with its scepticism of UN guarantees. However, the Super Powers could make their commitment more credible by also acting outside UN auspices: they, together with Britain, France (or possibly others of the Nine)[28] and representatives of Eastern Europe, if judged necessary for reasons of political balance, could extend a political guarantee, possibly in the form of a Declaration. The advantage of such a multilateral guarantee was foreseen by the Brookings Report. In practical terms, this would amount to a commitment to be undertaken by the above powers when a Middle East Peacy Treaty is signed, to guarantee both the borders of Israel and its neighbours, and the various agreements in the settlement. These would include those relating to DMZs and limitations of forces and arms.

Under this political guarantee, the Super Powers and, say, Britain and France, would be free to act if either a Chinese veto or the inability of the United Nations to reach a decision prevented quick action. But how could such guarantees be implemented? As discussed in the following chapters, the signatories of the Declaration should undertake to exercise various economic and

71

military sanctions that could be accomplished externally to the area. Thus, the need for difficult active Super Power cooperation could be avoided. In the event of breaches of the settlement, obligations could be carried out immediately. If the guarantors were unable to decide on joint action, then each could fulfil its obligations in conformity with the Declaration, but within the 'agreed ground rules'.

Super Power Participation in Safeguards:

An unambiguous practical commitment to take part in safeguarding the frontiers agreed in a Middle East Peace Treaty would lend further credibility to a political declaration along these lines: it would increase the stakes of the Super Powers in being seen to observe the agreements. Variants of the idea that the two Super Powers should police the frontiers have emerged intermittently since 1970. The suggestion that Super Power involvement should be more substantial than a verbal promise has stimulated fierce discussion. But the possibility must not be ruled out. It may well be that international circumstances demand that decision-makers take a bold, untried step that would firmly commit Washington and Moscow to uphold a final settlement. Inevitably, the number of ways in which the Super Powers could participate practically is reduced by the attitudes of the two Powers and local parties, as well as by the practical difficulties of Super Power cooperation already discussed.

Washington

The idea of joint Super Power involvement on the ground in a practical security arrangement was first broached publicly in a Californian White House briefing on 26 August 1970.[29] As for the precise form of cooperation, it was not clear whether the proposal was for a Two Power or a more widely representative force, or whether it would be outside UN auspices. However, opposition from Israelis, the Arab confrontation states (except King Hussein, who favoured the idea), the UN Secretariat and Capitol Hill compelled President Nixon to disassociate himself from the idea and, by the end of 1970, Secretary of State Rogers had ruled out a joint peace-keeping force.[30] Instead, the United

States was willing to participate in an international one. And, in March 1971, this was confirmed when the Four Powers reached a consensus that a UN peace-keeping force should include Four Power contingents.

After the October War, the Administration's thinking changed. Both unilateral and joint American–Soviet guarantees to supplement any settlement came under consideration, but the Administration became more 'dubious' about stationing Super Power forces on the ground.[31] In this, the United States was influenced to a large extent by the Soviet Union's call for a joint American–Soviet military intervention in the Middle East in 1973. The Administration apparently saw no need and no advantage in formalising the Soviet presence in this way. Consequently, when it came to the formation of UN Emergency Force II (UNEF II), the Administration firmly insisted that the Super Powers reject participation in the force. By 1976, senior officials were still cautious about direct participation even after a settlement. Whilst these officials conceded that the Soviet Union could not be politically excluded from a settlement and must therefore be a 'partner to the peace', they saw little advantage in extending active cooperation further.[32] Preferring minimum Super Power involvement, hesitant of any arrangement which might freeze the Super Powers into feared dangerous confrontation and influenced by the climate of opinion reflected at the Sinai Hearings, officials ruled out military involvement.

Nevertheless, there appears to be no opposition in American foreign policy circles to the idea that American and Soviet officers could be attached in an administrative capacity to UN peace-keeping forces, or that the present Super Power participation in the UN Truce Supervision Organisation (UNTSO) could be extended to other frontiers.[33] Also, despite the strong feelings expressed at the 1975 Sinai Hearings, the possibility remains of extending the American monitoring role to other fronts in the context of an overall settlement. If such an American presence should be required to bring about an agreement, it seems that Congress would not object. The main provisos are likely to be that the presence be limited to monitoring demilitarisation (ground surveillance, aerial reconnaissance) and be accompanied by a network of mutual security arrangements.

Soviet statements on guarantees have been cautious but consistent. Since October 1970, the approach has been that DMZs and guarantees by the Four Powers or the UN Security Council should be part of a 'package' solution.[34] Whilst the principles of a settlement are open to discussion, the details of a security arrangement are not, at least not before the conditions of a settlement are met.[35]

It is often inferred in the West that the Soviets are hesitant to commit themselves to any detailed guarantee plan which could affect their position adversely in the Arab world. But, in fact, they have gone further in their public declarations than their Arab clients would wish. First, the Soviet Union talks of the primary political responsibility of the Super Powers as Co-Chairmen of the Geneva Conference to get the negotiating process moving – 'There is nothing as important as Super Power cooperation', Soviet sources say. Second, the Soviets want to take part in safeguards and guarantees, whatever these might be, on equal terms with the United States, and talk of their willingness to do so. Contrary to what many Western officials say, the Soviet Union has probably been more explicit in its public statements on guarantees than most countries in the West. Indeed, it shows every sign of being ready to carry appropriate responsibilities in guaranteeing the security of Israel as well as of Israel's neighbours after a peace settlement.

Typical of the Soviets' line was Yevgeny Primakov's article in *Pravda* of 15 October 1970. This stipulated the need for DMZs on 'either side' of the frontiers giving 'no advantage' to either side and incorporating restrictions of a 'purely military character'. It called for 'the introduction of UN troops at a number of points and direct guarantees from the Big Four Permanent Members of the Security Council or the UN Security Council itself'.[36] Similarly, at the Four Power Talks, the Soviets spoke of Security Council guarantees with UN observers or troop contingents to be stationed 'on both sides of the border'. It was suggested that the permanent members 'might' contribute troops. Moscow's official endorsement of the idea of Four Power guarantees came in President Leonid Brezhnev's speech in March 1971, when he said that 'the USSR was prepared to join other powers who are permanent members of the Security Council in providing international guarantees for a political settlement in the Middle East'.[37]

After the October War, the Soviet Union made declarations of its willingness to cooperate in international guarantees of the security of all states and peoples of the Near East once a settlement had been agreed. The most precise was Foreign Minister Gromyko's explicit statement on 23 April 1975 in Moscow before the Syrian Foreign Minister, offering Israel the 'strictest guarantees' with the participation (under an appropriate agreement) of the Soviet Union, once Israel had withdrawn from all occupied territory. Since then, the urgency of a settlement and the Soviets' insistence on an equal peace-making and peace-keeping role are said by informed Soviet sources to have led to an apparent adjustment in their policy, as demonstrated by further references to guarantees for Israel.[38]

Although recent statements indicate that Moscow's policy on the substance of a settlement – Israeli withdrawal from all territories, Palestinian self-determination, and security for all states – remains unaltered, they contain some more reassurances for Israel. The government statement of 28 April 1976 which stressed that the elements of a settlement described above were 'organically inter-connected', referred to Israeli withdrawal from Arab territories occupied in 1967.[39] Some Israelis thought this an important step, because it seemed to preclude a demand for return to the 1947 partition lines.[40] Similarly, the October 1976 plan, published by Tass and delivered to all the main protagonists, named Israel specifically as one of the states to be guaranteed, while all Arab states still hesitated to talk even of recognition.[41] However, Soviet academics say there will be no Soviet offer of guarantees until Israel has withdrawn from the occupied territories.

As for the purpose of guarantees, the Soviets do not talk in terms of 'compensating' for Israeli withdrawal or 'supplementing' mutual security commitments contained in a settlement.[42] Instead, informed Soviet sources talk of guarantees creating a 'peaceful atmosphere' when local powers still remain suspicious of one another and that they should be extended only 'if the contracting parties so desire'.[43]

For the Soviets, it is political parity with the United States that matters most when it comes to guarantees. Apparently, they do not want an 'institutionalised role' on the ground, which they fear might risk their troops becoming 'hostages' in an area which is not under Super Power control. However, this anxiety could change once a settlement is negotiated. What they do want is a political say equal to that of Washington in all parts of the peace process.[44] As Brezhnev warned in March 1977, 'The Soviet Union, as co-chairman of the Geneva Conference and a state situated in direct proximity to the area in question, has its own opinion on the main principles and directions of a future peace settlement'.[45] In fact, Moscow had already demonstrated in January 1977 that it could not be counted on to cooperate if excluded from the peace-making process. It decided to withhold its share of the cost of the UN peace-keeping force resulting from the 1975 Sinai Interim Agreement on the grounds that it was not involved in negotiations leading to the Agreement. Explaining the move, the Soviet Ambassador at the United Nations said: 'We cannot bear the financial responsibility for measures taken without our participation'.[46] Just as insistently, the Soviets maintain that any peace-keeping force must have the Security Council as its 'collective head', as is now the case in the area.

Informed Soviet sources, speculating about the implementation of guarantees, confirm an 'obvious change' in Soviet thinking now that China is a permanent member of the Security Council. A political guarantee outside the United Nations might be easier to realise than a Security Council one.[47] And Brezhnev made this point in his March 1977 speech: '... the terms of the peace settlement could be guaranteed ... by the United Nations Security Council, or, perhaps, by individual Powers, for instance, the Soviet Union, the United States, France and Britain'.

The Brezhnev speech was also important because it elaborated on how safeguards could be practically implemented. Either UN forces or observers could be stationed in DMZs for a 'clearly specified period of time'. And in an unusual reference to direct Soviet participation, Brezhnev proposed that the guarantor states could have their observers in the UN contingents.[48] Since 1973, a precedent exists with thirty-six Russian observers alongside the American observers in UNTSO. The Soviets' preferred option, according to a senior Soviet diplomat, is that the UN peace-keeping force should be made up of non-aligned and Third World components. An observer non-combatant role for the Super Powers, with or without Britain and France, would not be incompatible with this.

The Soviets' cautious approach on the form that guarantees and safeguards might take reflects their concern to keep options open and to remain disentangled, and an awareness of potential political cost in terms of their relations with the Palestinians if they do not. But once matters of substance are settled, Moscow is likely to demand an equal role with Washington. And if the Americans agree, in a final settlement, to play a civilian monitoring role, possibly in addition to a UN observer one, the Soviets would insist that they do the same.

Summary – A Non-Combatant Super Power Role?

Although the Soviets' influence has been eroded in the Middle East, perhaps temporarily, they show no sign of accepting less than political parity. Nor need they. As an important source of arms and aid, and as a diplomatic counter to the United States, they remain a crucial factor in the Arab–Israeli equation.[49] If America does not persuade Israel to withdraw, the Arabs could turn in earnest to the Russians for support. Besides, Washington needs the Soviet Union to underwrite the settlement and to maintain arms limitation and demilitarisation agreements if they are to be able to preserve regional stability in the event of a crisis.

Fearful of the risks of Super Power confrontation inherent in the Arab–Israeli conflict, Moscow wants to cooperate with Washington. This could bring both the political parity Moscow seeks, together with prestige and a consolidation of détente. But the degree of potential cooperation is limited by practical difficulties. This in turn circumscribes the scope for potential direct co-management of the area by the Super Powers. Most feasible would be political commitments by both Super Powers to guarantee borders and DMZs together with 'passive' and symbolic forms of cooperation in safeguards on the ground.

The only convincing safeguard from the Israeli point of view would involve an American presence, and for reasons described, the Soviets would want to participate with the Americans. Within the above limits, one form of Super Power cooperation on the ground might be their participation in passive UN peace-keeping forces on those fronts where these forces might be deployed. Alternatively, if the reluctance of the Super Powers or fierce opposition from the local parties precluded this option, an unobtrusive non-combatant Super Power presence would be necessary. Such 'indirect' forms of Super Power cooperation might include a UN observer presence and possibly a civilian monitoring one.[50] The Super Powers could be attached in this latter capacity either to traditional UN peace-keeping forces or to guarantor forces (see p. 112) with a wider mandate if these were established on the West Bank and Gaza Strip and on the Israeli–Lebanese border.

In the crucial area of arms limitations, cooperation might involve the same kind of restraint as has been accepted in previous arms limitation agreements such as the SALT agreement.

[1] Interview data.

[2] Interview data. A senior French diplomat commented that if the Russians participated on the ground, they would become 'prisoners of their new conservative role which would limit their scope for political manoeuvre'.

[3] Soviet pilots and missile crews were killed during the War of Attrition. See William B. Quandt, 'Soviet Policy in the October Middle East War 1', *International Affairs*, Vol. 53, No. 3, July 1977, p. 378, Royal Institute of International Affairs, London. The US suffered casualties in the 'Liberty' incident in 1967 without reacting.

[4] In February 1977, some PLO leaders were sceptical about the desire of America for peace because of its apparent reluctance to pressurise Israel, despite the obvious compromises the Arab states had made during 1976 to modify their stance. For the Arab governments and the PLO, the reputation of the US will stand or fall on whether it is prepared to put pressure on Israel when the time comes. But see Lawrence L. Whetten, who talks of a 'firm American commitment' to the settlement process. 'The Arab–Israeli Dispute: Great Power Behaviour', *Adelphi Paper*, No. 128, IISS, London, Winter 1976/77, p. 43.

[5] A similar view has been put by Walter Laqueur. See his article, 'Is Peace Possible in the Middle East?', *Commentary*, Vol. 61, No. 3, March 1976.

[6] According to *The Guardian* (London), 23 February 1977, 'Moscow is said to be advising the PLO leadership to show flexibility'. And in May 1977, the Soviet Union is said to have informed the United States through diplomatic sources that the PLO is prepared to accept Resolution 242 if Israel simultaneously recognises the right of the Palestinian people to a national homeland. *Financial Times* (London), 10 May 1977.

[7] Interview data.

[8] The nearest Moscow is known to have come to entering into documentary commitments are the Treaties of Friendship and Cooperation with Egypt in May

1971 and with Iraq in April 1972. I am indebted to Peter Mangold for his thoughtful contribution to this discussion of Soviet commitments in the Middle East.

[9] The erosion of the political relationship between Egypt and the Soviet Union raises questions about Soviet behaviour in a future war. But the same would apply to more formal political ties.

[10] See also Jon D. Glassman, *Arms for the Arabs*, The Johns Hopkins University Press, Baltimore and London, 1975, pp. 144–145.

[11] Whether the Soviet Union was or was not guilty of violating agreements depends on one's expectations and definition of the requirements of détente. The two agreements cited are: i) the third article of the Joint Statement of Principles Governing Relations between the Soviet Union and the United States (29 May 1972), in which the two parties committed themselves 'to do everything in their power so that conflicts or situations will not arise which would serve to increase international tensions'; and, ii) the agreement of 22 June 1973, in which the signatories pledged themselves to 'act in such a manner as to prevent the development of situations capable of causing a dangerous exacerbation of their relations'. See Quandt, op. cit., p. 378, f.2.

[12] *USIS*, No. 217, 22 November 1973.

[13] Although the armed sections of the PLO are known to possess Soviet-made equipment, it is likely it came to them via third parties, e.g. Libya.

[14] The Soviet Union's relations with the PLO are partly governed by its concern to counter China's backing of the PFLP, a party which they consider adventurist and Trotskyite.

[15] See, generally, Galia Golan, 'The Soviet Union and the PLO', *Adelphi Paper*, No. 131, IISS, London, Winter 1976.

[16] One of the reasons for President Sadat's break with the Russians was that Brezhnev put détente with the United States first.

[17] Interview data.

[18] President Sadat suspected the Super Powers had reached a tacit understanding on limiting arms supplies. Later he said, 'It was clear that the stalemate – no peace, no war – suited the Superpowers. There was some agreement between them about the level of arms supplies'. Quoted in *The Sunday Times* (London), 9 December 1973.

[19] *International Herald Tribune*, 1 September 1970.

[20] See N. A. Pelcovits, 'Security Guarantees in a Middle East Settlement', Foreign Policy Research Institute, *Sage Publications*, 1976, p. 64, n. 85.

[21] The 1972 Joint Statement of Principles (op. cit.) might be cited as another example. But some maintain that the Soviet Union violated this agreement in 1973. See *The Times* (London), 3 October 1977 for the text of the American–Soviet statement.

[22] President Nixon supplied arms to Israel in 1972. Soviet behaviour in 1973, in the eyes of many observers, undermined the 1972 Joint Statement of Principles (op. cit).

[23] Interview data.

[24] One senior Israeli diplomat pointed out that the Soviets could land in Haifa purportedly to 'defend' Israel against Arab attack.

[25] See Pelcovits, op. cit., pp. 15, 37.

[26] When interviewed, French experts argued that the value of deterrence would

lie in the Force Commander's mandate to observe, defend his force and retaliate against incidents: for example, if tanks of either side crossed any border, the force should have the authority to shoot at those tanks.

[27] If the local parties accepted the peace settlement, China could be expected to abstain, rather than to veto, such a resolution.

[28] This is problematic because the various members of the Nine would have both political and constitutional arguments working against the practical role suggested here.

[29] *USIS*, 27 August 1970; *The Observer* (London), 30 August 1970. Unexpectedly, Senator Javits had speculated that American and Russian 'peace-keeping forces' would be required to reinforce a Middle East settlement and give the UN forces 'some muscle'. Interview with CBS News, 9 August 1970, *Congressional Record*, Vol. 116, No. 140, Washington, 13 August 1970. Senator Fulbright, Chairman of the Foreign Relations Committee, had said in a speech titled *Old Myths and New Realities – The Middle East* (delivered in the Senate on 24 August 1970) that it might be a good idea if Americans and Russians offered their Middle East clients certain military guarantees.

[30] *The New York Times*, 24 December 1970; *Jerusalem Post Weekly*, 28 December 1970. The idea, not revived by the Administration, was taken up by George Ball in 1974. To prevent a Balkan-like situation involving the Super Powers in a nuclear confrontation and to test détente, the Super Powers should extend joint guarantees which might be accompanied by 'joint Soviet–American patrols of buffer areas'. See *Trialogue*, Winter 1974–75, No. 6, and George W. Ball, 'The Looming War in the Middle East and How to Avert It', *Atlantic Monthly*, January 1975, p. 10. The Trilateral Commission endorsed the idea of joint Super Power guarantees, but three of its members went further by advocating a Super Power presence. Automatic involvement of the Super Powers would necessitate crisis management. See Zbigniew Brzezinski, François Duchêne and Kiichi Saeki, 'Peace in an International Framework', *Foreign Policy*, Summer 1975. Other formulas for active Super Power cooperation have been talked about. Former Under Secretary George C. McGhee proposed that the Four Powers should be ready to supplement a UN guarantee of frontiers with denial of arms, blockade and, in extreme cases, air action based outside the area. If the UN failed to stop aggression, each power would carry out its interpretation of its obligations under a declaration – within the agreed ground rules designed to prevent direct confrontation in the area. 'Peace with a Guarantee', *The Washington Post*, 14 January 1974.

[31] *USIS*, 17 December 1973. Before taking office, Vice-President Ford had declared before two Congressional Committees on 6 December 1973 that he did not think the United States should enter into a firm treaty with Israel or commit itself to sending troops to the Middle East.

[32] Interview data. But those interviewed generally supported the view expressed by Secretary Kissinger in his Cincinnatti speech of 16 September 1975 – that the US was prepared to work with the Soviet Union in search of a final peace.

[33] UNTSO supervised the 1948 truce in Palestine; serviced armistice agreements from 1949; supervised cease-fire lines on the Suez Canal and Golan Heights, 1967–73; and assisted UNEF II and UN Disengagement Observer Force (UNDOF) since 1973. In 1973, the Soviet Union asked for 36 of its officers to participate as UN Military Observers (UNMOs) and American participation was then also brought up to 36.

[34] *Soviet News*, 20 October 1970.

[35] Interview data.

[36] *Soviet News*, 20 October 1970. This was a new version of a plan originally presented to the Americans in December 1969; see *The New York Times*, 13 January 1970 for text.

[37] Report of the Central Committee of the CPSU to the 24th Congress of the CPSU on 30 March 1971.

[38] Foreign Minister Gromyko's conciliatory gesture was interpreted as an attempt to seek Israeli cooperation to meet at Geneva with the PLO and is said to have followed informal Israeli–Soviet discussions. *The New York Times*, 24 April 1975. For reports of explicit Soviet support for the inviolability of Israel within its 1967 borders, see also *The Daily Telegraph* (London), 12 April 1975, *The Times* (London), 3 October 1975, and *The New York Times*, 3 October 1975.

[39] *Soviet News*, 4 May 1976.

[40] *Jerusalem Post Weekly*, 22 June 1976.

[41] *Le Monde*, 3–4 October 1976.

[42] One exception was Gromyko's reference to 'commitments within international law taken upon themselves by the sides' as the 'best guarantee' of their mutual security. Statement by Gromyko at the Peace Conference to the Middle East, Tass in English, 21 December 1973, Foreign Broadcast Information Service, Soviet Union, 26 December 1973, p. F3. Cited in Pelcovits, op. cit., p. 33.

[43] Interview data. See also Brezhnev's speech to the 16th Congress of Soviet Trade Unions, 21 March 1977, Summary of World Broadcasting, 22 March 1977.

[44] Interview with a senior Soviet diplomat.

[45] Brezhnev's speech, op. cit.

[46] *International Herald Tribune*, 8–9 January 1977. But, significantly, the Soviet Union did not take exception to the principle of collective financial responsibility which was one of the major achievements in the establishment of UNEF II.

[47] Interview data.

[48] Brezhnev's speech, op. cit.

[49] Peter Mangold, 'The Soviet Record in the Middle East', *Survival*, Vol. XX, No. 3, IISS, London, May/June 1978.

[50] The October 1977 joint Super Power statement draws attention to the willingness of both parties to participate in the observance of the terms of the settlement as well as in international guarantees, subject to the Super Powers' own constitutional processes. *The Times* (London), 3 October 1977.

5. BORDERS:
FROM SAFEGUARDS TO
SECURITY GUARANTEES

Consensus and Compromise

As discussed in Chapter 2, the position of the Israeli Government and its Arab neighbours on a peace settlement are far apart. Egypt and other moderate Arab states insist on full Israeli withdrawal to 1967 borders and the right of Palestinian self-determination. These principles are a far cry from the Begin Plan, the chief points of which are: maintenance of Israeli civilian settlements and a military presence in Sinai and on the West Bank and Gaza Strip; and a limited form of internal 'self-rule', *not* full self-determination, for the Palestinians.

Finding a compromise formula may well depend on the security measures that can be devised to meet Israeli security requirements, and on the role that outside powers are prepared to play. The security measures open to discussion will be early warning safeguards, such as DMZs, limited armament zones and surveillance techniques; international guarantor forces and enforcement techniques; and external security guarantees.

The Carter Administration has been influenced in its Middle East policy by the Brookings Report. Brookings proposes compromise solutions on key issues. The central proposition is that although the necessary inducement for the parties to agree would be that all aspects of the settlement should be spelt out in a 'package deal', implementation would take place in agreed stages. The idea is that 'particular steps of withdrawal' would be 'matched with security measures and steps in the establishment of peaceful and normal relations'.[1]

During 1977, the Carter Administration defined three key elements of a final settlement, which might take up to eight years to implement: full Israeli withdrawal to approximately 1967 borders; a full peace; and establishment of a Palestinian homeland. Then, in July 1977, President Carter made clear that he favoured a

Palestinian entity federated with Jordan, rather than a state.[2]

President Carter attempted to clarify his territorial and security proposals. He made a distinction on the one hand between permanent and internationally-recognised borders, involving only 'minor adjustments to the 1967 borders' to which the Israelis would ultimately withdraw; and on the other hand 'defence lines' beyond these which might continue to exist for a time. He elaborated on the Brookings' 'security measures'. There might, he suggested, be 'extensions of Israeli defence capability' beyond legal borders, but he hinted that alternatively there might be other safeguards: international forces, a broad belt of demilitarisation, or monitoring stations (electronics and personnel outposts) as in Sinai.[3]

The central importance of DMZs in a comprehensive settlement is internationally accepted. UN Security Council Resolution 242 affirms the need for DMZs 'for guaranteeing the territorial inviolability and political independence of every state in the area', and Brookings acknowledges that peace agreements will probably contain provision for 'rather extensive demilitarized zones, to be supervised by the UN forces or observers or by joint commissions of the parties, and to be maintained for periods of time prescribed in the agreements'. The Russians, too, publicly advocated in their peace proposals of March 1977 the creation of DMZs; but on condition that these are 'without unilateral advantage for any side', on both sides of agreed borders with UN emergency forces or observers, possibly including Russian, American, British and French representatives, and 'for some clearly specified period of time'.[4]

By their acceptance of Resolution 242 and in public statements since, the Egyptians, Israelis and Syrians do acknowledge the need for DMZs.[5] In January 1978, Yassir Arafat publicly proposed that borders of an independent Palestinian state should be policed by an international peace-keeping force. The implication here is that the PLO recognises that at least part of their proposed state should be demilitarised.[6] But positions are far apart on where DMZs should be, how long they should be in place, and on the security measures that should accompany them.[7]

Demilitarised Zones

The chief question is: how would the demilitarisation of certain designated areas be guaranteed?

Just as terrain and population-density affect the gravity of threats across borders, so they determine the efficacy and suitability of security measures. In the case of Israel's future borders with Egypt and Syria (and possibly with Lebanon), it is imaginable that the early warning system (demilitarised buffer zones, peace-keeping forces, electronic monitoring systems and air reconnaissance) at present operating in Sinai could be adapted to meet their different security requirements. In addition to their own surveillance, the Israelis would probably insist that any tactical early warning system should be manned by Americans, even if only as civilians. Should the Arab states then insist on a similar Soviet presence, this is not expected to raise serious problems. To these early warning safeguards would be added formal guarantees. If external guarantors failed to prevent battle through diplomatic threats, then prior commitments should oblige them to come to the aid of a threatened state.

For a number of reasons, it would not be difficult to render the Sinai frontier relatively safe against surprise attacks. Here, the desert and nomadic population make surveillance easy and the large areas available permit the armed forces of both sides to be separated. This reduces the likelihood of incidents and escalation and provides a limited deterrent against infiltration. The danger of surprise attack by ground forces of either side through any one of the four invasion corridors would be reduced by virtue of the width of the demilitarised buffer zone and other early warning devices. These would provide the parties to this border with sufficient early warning (time and space) to insist on a return to the *status quo ante* after a violation, or to mobilise and fight ultimately in self-defence. In this event, both Israel and Egypt could provide sufficient military forces to defend themselves until their guarantors sent them aid. To this extent, the frontier is self-enforcing and the Super Power role would be limited to that of mediator in diplomacy and to guarantor in time of war.

This kind of system, dependent on space and local party military strength, could be established, but with greater difficulty, on the Golan. Admittedly, the shorter distances in this area make minor military engagements between local parties more possible and facilitate surprise attack. And the presence of a civilian population, albeit small, makes it easier for fedayeen to infiltrate unobserved. So, the risk of small incidents increases. Since early warning safeguards could not provide the necessary military security for either side, the need for formal international guarantees would inevitably be greater. But, provided a comprehensive settlement is negotiated, thereby removing the possibility of a surprise attack on the Egyptian frontier, the difficulties of the Golan are thought to be surmountable.

It is difficult to say precisely what security problems the Israeli–Lebanese border would present after a peace settlement. But the system described above, depending on DMZs and local party military strength, is unlikely to be applicable. On this northern frontier, the problem is not so much the threat of surprise attack on Israel by Lebanon or *vice versa*. This is because the Lebanese (or Syrian) and Israeli armies could be separated; and because Israeli and Lebanese aerial reconnaissance would provide the necessary early warning. But, this northern border does run through a fairly densely populated area with Israelis and Palestinians living on either side. Within south Lebanon there are also tense relations between the Christians and the Palestinians and their leftist allies. Admittedly, assuming a full Israeli withdrawal on other fronts and the creation of a Palestinian 'homeland', the security problem currently posed by the Palestinian armed presence in south Lebanon would be mitigated: many fedayeen would choose to live in the new Palestinian entity. But others, amongst them the irredentists, dissatisfied with a compromise settlement and the creation of a West Bank entity, would surely remain – making south Lebanon a base for future operations against Israel. Moreover, those Palestinian refugees choosing to stay in south Lebanon would provide cover for the guerrillas. With Israelis and Palestinians living side-by-side in the border area, the Israelis would continue to fear commando raids; and the south Lebanese would in turn fear Israeli reprisals.

With Beirut unable to exercise military control over the south, Israel's answer to the terrorist threat, prior to a peace settlement, has been to combine its policy of retaliation with the creation of a *de facto* security zone policed by itself and the Maronite Christians. When these security measures were threatened in late 1977, Israel took the opportunity, in March 1978, to intervene massively in south Lebanon with the declared objective of establishing a six-mile-wide security belt. Since this action violated Lebanese sovereignty and was totally unacceptable to all Arabs and Palestinians, the challenge was for outside powers to provide alternative military control. This they did by despatching UNIFIL a few days later 'to confirm the withdrawal of Israeli forces', 'to restore international peace and security' and 'to assist the Government of Lebanon in ensuring the return of its effective authority in the area'.

Whether UNIFIL will succeed in its tasks is still uncertain (much depends on the cooperation of the PLO and leftist militia, and this in turn depends on the acceptance by the Christians of UNIFIL): but some tentative remarks about the possible effectiveness of a UNIFIL-type force on this border after a peace settlement are offered on pages 113–120.

The case of the West Bank is also altogether different to the Sinai. Assuming a full Israeli withdrawal, a Sinai-type early warning system could not possibly be made effective between Israel and a new Palestinian entity. The security problems posed by the populated West Bank and Gaza Strip are of a different order and are much more intractable. The difficulty would not so much concern the unlikely threat of conventional attack on Israel by Jordan (supported, say, by Syria or Iraq) or *vice versa*. This is because Jordan and Israel could agree to separate their armies, whatever the political future of the West Bank, and because their own aerial reconnaissance would continue to provide the necessary early warning. These countries, therefore, could ultimately depend on their own national forces to defend themselves against each other. The problem is rather that the frontier running between Israel and a Palestinian entity would be militarily indefensible. It would not matter whether the West Bank and Gaza Strip were made into an independent state or an autonomous unit linked to Jordan, or whether they were placed under a UN trusteeship while moving towards self-determination. The fact is that any frontier would run through densely populated areas, between neighbouring fields and near to militarily vulnerable areas such as Israel's narrow waistline, or a Palestinian entity's equally vulnerable Gaza Strip. Moreover, Jerusalem, whatever its political future, would lie as a hostage to fortune where the borders of a Palestinian 'homeland' and Israel would meet. The city might not only become a focus for civil and communal strife, but would also be a potential target for artillery fire from all sides, including Jordan.

Unlike Israel's genuinely international frontiers, this border would approximate the old 'green line' established at the cease-fire in 1948 between the two communities living together in Palestine until then. Thus, this border would present special political problems too. After all, two peoples with claimants amongst them – the Likud Party and the PLO – to land on either side of the frontier would be living cheek-by-jowl. So, the danger of renewed fedayeen incursions, with more sophisticated weapons, would be directly related to the threat of Israeli reprisal raids. The danger would be one of small incidents escalating, possibly even to include neighbour states.

But here is the rub. Given that there is no distance (as on Israel's other frontiers) to separate the populations of Israel and the new Palestinian entity, the frontier could not be militarily defensible. Just as Israelis would live in constant fear if the West Bank and Gaza Strip were not militarily controlled, so Palestinians would know that they could never hope to achieve a military balance with Israel and could not therefore act in their own self-defence.

The Israeli answer to this problem is that they should themselves retain the military control of the West Bank and Gaza Strip. They would seek to keep these areas demilitarised, acting along the lines of the Allon, Dayan or Begin Plans. However, as discussed earlier, these Plans are politically unacceptable to all Palestinians and would, in any case, intensify any irredentist tendencies that they might harbour.

So alternative proposals for the military control of a Palestinian entity's borders and level of arms need, therefore, to be explored. The question is: could outside powers keep these borders secure, and how? Of all Israel's borders, it is generally agreed that the West Bank and Gaza Strip present the toughest problems because Israeli and Arab demands concerning their future are quite irreconcilable. Two security plans are therefore described later in this chapter. The first is advocated by a number of American academics close to State Department thinking. The second consists of a bold innovation which would subordinate local party guarantees to outside military protection, with the Super Powers playing a crucial symbolic role. However, the introduction of an international force with a mandate to fight would require an external administration. The question of which international authority could best administer the military control of these areas should therefore be seriously examined. But, before looking at what form the protection of a future Palestinian entity's borders might take, the security problems of Israel's other borders, which can be properly dealt with by up-dated existing techniques, are examined.

I THE SINAI AND THE GOLAN

1. Political and Security Requirements

President Sadat has intimated that, provided Egypt has sovereignty over all Sinai, there could be a phased withdrawal over, say, eighteen months in Sinai. He has said that security provisions should include: DMZs on a reciprocal basis (taking into consideration the difference between the depths of Egypt and Israel); early warning stations for Egypt and Israel on their own territory respectively; a UN presence along the border, in the DMZs and possibly at Sharm-el-Shaikh; areas of limited armaments; a zone in Sinai to which the Egyptian forces would return; and freedom of navigation in the Gulf of Aqaba.[8] Sadat has stressed that Israeli civilian settlements and a military presence in Sinai after withdrawal would violate Egyptian sovereignty. Furthermore, the presence of Israeli civilians manning an Israeli early warning station on UN-flagged territory would not be acceptable even in the context of a phased withdrawal. But this might conceivably be negotiable.

Israeli demands, based on a phased withdrawal over three to five years, include: a demilitarised buffer zone from northern Sinai to the Giddi and Mitla Passes, which would provide a measure of strategic depth that Israel would otherwise lack; a UN presence in the buffer zone; the retention of permanent Israeli settlements on Egyptian territory at Sharm-el-Shaikh and in the Rafiah Salient. These to be administratively connected to the State of Israel and defended (in the original proposal) by Israeli ground forces; areas of limited forces and armaments; and Israel's right to keep three air-fields – two in north Sinai and one near Sharm-el-Shaikh.[9]

The Sadat diplomacy has produced these statements concerning the practical implementation of security measures in Sinai. But if this initiative is to be prevented from running into the ground, some progress must be made on finding a compromise formula for the West Bank acceptable to Israelis and Arabs alike.[10] Only then are the negotiating terms of the Israelis and the Syrians on the question of the Golan likely to be further elaborated.

2. Future Demilitarised Zones: Proposals

It is assumed here that if they are to be credible and effective, DMZs must be free of all arms, manpower and infrastructure of the hostile parties.

In *Sinai*, where geography permits, the DMZ should be wider than the range of heavy mortars and artillery.[11] Then, the zone would serve as a true buffer – reducing risks of incidents and infiltration, providing early warning against surprise attack and building confidence between the parties.

The Israelis might eventually agree to a phased withdrawal to 1967 lines and to leave Sharm-el-Shaikh, provided Egyptian forces did not move in to take their place.[12] Israel's security could be best assured by the total demilitarisation of territory relinquished by Israel since the 1975 Sinai Interim Agreement; the Israeli Government regards this as crucial in order to establish a balance of forces between Israel and Egypt.[13] Egypt would keep those forces already permitted in Sinai. Furthermore, to meet the Egyptian demand for reciprocity, when Israel has withdrawn behind internationally-recognised borders, a token strip of Israeli territory should be demilitarised.[14] Then, in order to deny access to intruders, two sensor lines should be created: one east of the north–south road in West Sinai and another in the Israeli DMZ. There would be UN check-points at all east–west crossings.

The above option would involve enlarging the present buffer zone on the eastern side as far as the Israeli side of the international border by the end of the withdrawal period. Israel could derive satisfaction because Egyptian forces would not be permitted to move further east; Egypt could be compensated for this if the odd Egyptian platoon was allowed to carry out patrols in the DMZ at well-publicised intervals.

However, the size of the DMZ will be subject to intense negotiation. The Egyptians may insist on moving their troops further east (even beyond the Passes) or introducing additional forces. Should demilitarisation of the total area from which the IDF eventually withdraws be unacceptable to the Egyptians, then a formula involving a phased 'movement' of the buffer zone, always at least 40–50 kilometres wide, could be devised. On the Egyptian side, the existing limited-forces-and-armaments zone (LFA) would increase in size as the buffer zone 'moved' eastwards. The Egyptian LFA would be necessary so that SAMs, tanks, artillery and troops of both sides would be separated by at least sixty kilometres – an added measure against surprise attack, as well as a confidence-building measure.

In both the above cases, the wide band of demilitarisation would have an important deterrent effect: effective ground attack across Sinai would be impossible for either side. If the Egyptians attacked, their forces would be exposed to the full weight of an Israeli mobile campaign. SAM air defence support would necessarily be dispersed, less mobile and more exposed to Israeli air attack. The Israeli air-force, operating close to Israel's borders, would suffer less interference from Egyptian defence and ground forces. And in the event of an Israeli attack, the Egyptians would also stand to gain: Israeli forces deployed in Sinai would be fully exposed. Both sides would get earlier warning if they maintained surveillance stations and carried out photo-reconnaissance (see pp. 97–99).

On the *Golan*, where distances are shorter, a negotiated DMZ will provide crucial but only limited early warning and other sophisticated technical safeguards become more necessary.[15] Though themselves costly, the establishment of monitoring systems adapted to the confined area of the Golan would be cheap when compared with the cost of arms supplied to either side in war-time. The size of the zone would be negotiable, but the same principle of at least a token reciprocal band of demilitarisation on Israeli territory should apply.

One possibility would be the creation of equally broad demilitarised areas on both sides of the 1967 border. Thus, on the Israeli side, the Hula Valley would be demilitarised and troops withdrawn to defensive positions on high ground west of the Jordan River; on the Syrian side, an equally broad band of the Heights would be demilitarised. The border, which would be internationally patrolled, would have a limited number of tightly controlled access points to safeguard against guerilla infiltration.

This arrangement would allow Israel to absorb an attack in the Jordan Valley, but would leave no strategic depth for Israel to move on to the offensive in order to drive the Syrian army off the Golan crest. Given this drawback, and the fact that a future battle would be fought in the Valley, where settlements would be precariously exposed, this arrangement would be surely unacceptable to Israel.

At present, Israel's positions on the Golan would permit it to fight a mobile tank battle on the plateau to prevent the Syrians gaining control of the crest before Israeli reserves reached it. But retention of Israeli forces on the Golan is unacceptable to the Syrians. Israel might, however, be persuaded to withdraw from the Heights if assured that a Syrian offensive would not reach the escarpment before the Israelis arrived with sufficient forces.

Because of the short distances involved, demilitarisation and present third party surveillance techniques alone would not provide Israel with the assured protection from a Syrian surprise attack that it seeks. Nevertheless, Israel's fear would have been considerably alleviated if it felt entirely safe from surprise attack from Egypt and if in addition to early warning safeguards it was provided with a formal guarantee of last resort. If so, what might be the best combination of security measures?

It is conceivable that the demilitarised area extend further east, possibly incorporating the present Syrian LFA. In order to seal the DMZ, one sensor line might be set up on high ground east of the present buffer zone and another at the base of the Golan escarpment. Both sensor lines could be manned by the United Nations (and possibly monitored by the Israelis and Syrians respectively from their own territory) and would be supplemented by UN check-points. Combined with these surveillance devices. providing early warning, there could be barriers such as mine-fields, tank-traps and fences which would serve to delay any Syrian advance.

In addition, there might be limited deployment in certain areas of Syrian troops and forces. But with the small distances involved, a Syrian LFA would be likely to take in the outskirts of its capital, Damascus, leaving it virtually defenceless. Syria would be unwilling to pay such a price in return for Israeli withdrawal down the Golan slopes.[16]

Though negotiations will be difficult, the very possibility of separating the confronting parties on the Golan, thus giving UN forces clear lines to observe and supervise, means the security problem is potentially surmountable, if only with ultimate guarantees from the parties' backers.

3. Safeguards:

Innovations in peace-keeping and new safeguards enhancing early warning in Sinai support the contention: 'There is hardly any limit to the alternative plans that might be devised for bringing technology into the process of reducing the opportunity for military attack across Arab–Israeli frontiers'.[17] Certainly, the success of the Sinai venture has restored the credibility of safeguards intended to warn against and deter surprise attack. These safeguards (DMZs, UN forces, unmanned electronic sensors, surveillance stations and air reconnaissance) can be taken as models for future security measures in Sinai, on the Golan, and possibly astride the Israeli–Lebanese border, provided they are improved and adapted to take account of certain weaknesses and longer term problems.

United Nations

For practical and juridical reasons, the principal aim of the UN forces could not be to fulfil the combat role of a 'collective security' force. First, no UN force could take on the armies of Israel and the Arab states, nor could it by itself prevent war. Second, member states are likely to object to setting up peace-keeping forces in the Middle East with an explicit mandate to use force offensively. Even if this political obstacle was overcome by extending the 'defensive capabilities' of UN forces, the use of the veto in the Security Council could still prevent enforcement action. This degree of uncertainty is critical for Israel, which therefore prefers not to put any trust in UN peace-keeping forces as a guarantee.

However, these factors would not circumscribe the ability of UN peace-keeping forces to serve as an effective buffer in DMZs on Israel's borders with Egypt and Syria.[18] President Carter has said that security measures should extend over five to eight years. However, we suggest that, in Sinai and on the Golan, security measures should continue for a further 'confidence-building' period – say, fifteen years in all – during which arms levels could be brought to a more stable balance. Subsequently, such measures could be re-assessed by the parties concerned – some might be discarded, some retained.

During those fifteen years, peace maintenance tasks would comprise: supervision of the phased withdrawal of Israeli forces to the boundaries defined in the settlement, including from DMZs in Israel, and of re-deployment of forces and armaments in LFAs; supervision of borders and of DMZs and LFAs; denial of access to the forces of either side to the DMZs.

In *Sinai*, at Sharm-el-Shaikh and in the Israeli DMZ too, the demilitarised areas would be under Egyptian and Israeli civilian administrations respectively. The UN force, aided by UN unarmed Military Observers (UNMOs), would maintain check-points and observation posts, undertake ground patrols along sensor lines and around and within buffer zones, and carry out sea patrols in inshore waters. On the *Golan*, UN tasks would be carried out much as at present. The Syrians and Israelis would insist that the demilitarised parts of their territory be under their own civil administration, and that a force, similar to the UN Disengagement Observer Force (UNDOF), comply with Syrian and Israeli laws and regulations.[19] If a peace settlement permits gradual civilian return as did the 1974 Disengagement Agreement, perhaps eventually extending to the Israeli 1967 borders (and even a provision for Israeli civilians to stay), the barring of entry to guerrillas would need to be efficient and skilful.

To fulfil the above tasks, the UN forces will need an efficient command structure. The crucial need will be a balance between: the requirement, currently in force, that all matters affecting the nature or effectiveness of the force, be referred to the Security Council for its decision (withdrawal of the force could only be decided by an affirmative vote of the Security Council itself); and, the Secretary General's authority over and responsibility for day-to-day running of the force within the terms of the mandate, in order to avoid delays, leaving the Security Council to deal with major policy issues.[20] The precise degree of authority to be allocated to the Secretary General will have to be negotiated, since the Russians and the French maintain that the Security Council itself must control operations and insist on this 'collective head'.

To facilitate the Secretary General's task, the Force Commanders responsible to him might be given directives approved by the Security Council covering the tasks of their particular forces.[21] In addition, given that the post-settlement peace-keeping tasks will be highly sensitive, the Secretary General could appoint a Special Representative (SRSG). He would be responsible for all UN political and economic matters affecting the presence of UN forces, including any special tasks that the Secretary General might give him in the context of negotiations with the local governments. There would also be a Chief Coordinator of Military Operations, as at present, who would be in overall charge.[22]

Composition of a politically-balanced and impartial UN force will be difficult because of practical and political constraints:[23] for instance, the issue of longer term mandates is controversial.[24] But the fact that UN forces should be operating in an atmosphere of 'normalisation' between local parties might influence contributors favourably.

There are other problems. Under present guide-lines, only the Security Council can withdraw a force during a mandate that it has itself authorised. But, at the end of a specified period, either party might withhold its consent to renewal. Current UNEF II and UNDOF mandates are short, and if the local parties withdraw their consent, as both Egypt and Syria have threatened to do in the past, it is difficult to visualise contingents staying on 'willy-nilly'. If the mandate were longer and the local parties withheld their cooperation, the present thinking is that the United Nations could not operate effectively against local opposition. Such uncertainty has tended to undermine the credibility of UN forces in the past.

To overcome this uncertainty, the United Nations could make a formal commitment for, say, fifteen years, leaving the question of extension to the end of the period. The host countries (Israel, Syria and Egypt) would negotiate mandate renewal dates, but mandates should be at least five years long. UN forces could only be removed at the request of both sides, not of either alone. And contributing states would be expected to undertake a firm commitment that their contingents would serve for a fixed period and according to a specified mandate.[25]

Given the vast areas to be controlled, the problems of manpower and financing rule out the possibility of significantly larger forces than existing ones. But what countries will be willing to contribute troops, possibly against domestic opposition, that are well-trained, reliable and noted for their impartiality? Not many Third World countries will have trained personnel to spare. But consistent with the principle of 'equitable geographic representation', adopted in 1973, Third World states, such as India, Pakistan and Nepal, together with NATO and Warsaw Pact countries, could contribute contingents. Although Security Council Resolution 340 of 25 October 1973 and the Protocol to the Agreement on Disengagement between Israeli and Syrian forces barred the participation of permanent members in UNEF II and UNDOF, France has contributed a contingent to UNIFIL and both Britain and France have indicated their willingness to participate in international forces established in a final settlement.[26] Therefore, these countries and other willing EEC countries might bring up numbers of trained personnel.[27] Those interviewed in the Middle East capitals were not concerned about the participation of former colonial powers in UN forces.

Because of the practical difficulties described in Chapter 4, the Super Powers would probably be excluded from the force itself. Also, according to senior American and Russian diplomats, both Washington and Moscow would prefer not to have their soldiers in the force. However, they would not apparently object to Americans and Soviets serving as individuals, in an administrative capacity, at UN Headquarters.[28]

Alternatively, to add to their vital symbolic support of the force, and to enhance Israel's now more favourable attitude to UN forces, America could provide additional UN observers or civilian monitors. As argued earlier, this would mean that the Soviets, who have indicated their willingness, would want to do likewise.[29] The Super Powers could also provide financial and logistic support for UN forces and air reconnaissance, as at present. The advantage would be that an international peace-keeping force with contingents from medium powers, including possibly Britain, France and Warsaw Pact countries, would then have the visible backing of the Super Powers. It is no easy matter for local parties to risk armed conflict with the United Nations. And it becomes the more irrational when their chief arms suppliers are demonstrably behind it. Neither Israel nor the Arabs could afford to ignore Super Power involvement in maintaining peace.

It seems probable, therefore, that UN troops will come from militarily-efficient and richer states outside the Middle East – West and East Europe, perhaps from Iran, and from the best trained forces of Third World and non-aligned countries.[30]

Verification

There would be two chief problems in establishing and maintaining an international surveillance system in a final settlement: logistics and technology. The United Nations does not at present have in the Middle East the technical expertise or the material resources to establish a complete border and area surveillance. Several years may be required to establish this capability. Meanwhile, the United Nations and willing individual countries will need to undertake inter-related surveillance activities on Middle East borders. For instance, those countries which have an acceptable capability could provide equipment and expertise for a particular portion of the overall problem. The aim would be to provide a credible border surveillance and verification system requiring a combination of unattended ground sensors, watch stations, optical and electro-optical observation devices, checkpoints, on-site inspections and photo-reconnaissance.

At present in *Sinai*, there are five levels of surveillance and verification activities. All serve as confidence-building measures (CBMs). In a final settlement, border and area surveillance systems in Sinai and on the Golan are likely to use, adapt and strengthen these techniques, most of which would also need to be used in any security plan devised for the West Bank and Gaza Strip and on the Israeli–Lebanese border.

i) UN officials concede that UN border and area verification techniques need to be improved. Various ways to do this might be: better strategic placement of check-points and observation posts; more frequent ground patrols around the buffer zone; more frequent and systematic inspection of buffer zones and LFAs – at random, rather than pre-scheduled; UN control of roads into and within the LFAs.[31] As for ground verification, UN officials say they need Night Observation Devices (NODs), long-range NODs and more helicopters to improve present inspection.

UN verification techniques will also need to be supplemented by photo-reconnaissance and by some means of monitoring movements into and out of restricted areas. Ground sensors and watch stations would need to monitor continuously all personnel crossing into DMZs or LFAs in Sinai and on the Golan. With the help of new infra-red observation devices along the sensor lines, concealment of movement and material would be much more difficult than in the past.[32]

ii) Local party surveillance stations in Sinai provide a precedent for similar arrangements for direct observation on Israeli borders with Syria and the Lebanon. Whether and where local early warning stations are placed in future DMZs will have to be negotiated. If Israel insisted on maintaining its early warning station in Sinai after withdrawal, Egypt might be prepared to compromise if this was manned by Israeli civilian personnel who could be ferried to and fro by UN helicopters. Egypt's own early warning station could be moved further east to the high ground of Jabal Hilal.

If the local parties could not accept this formula, there is another possibility: Egypt and Israel could maintain early warning stations in Israeli and Egyptian DMZs respectively. These might be manned by third parties, but Egypt and Israel could monitor movements from their own territory. This could apply equally well to early warning stations on the Golan.

The organised exchange of information between Israel and its neighbours could supplement such national intelligence-gathering. In the style of the Helsinki accords, each party could announce in advance planned military manoeuvres. Each could also notify the other when re-deploying forces – a valuable reassurance when moves occur in areas contiguous to LFAs and DMZs. As long as each party possessed equally sophisticated equipment and the process of unilateral collection and exchange of information remained immune from the tamperings of ill-wishers, intelligence-gathering would help build confidence between them.

iii) There would also be third party tactical early warning to monitor troop and tank movements where appropriate; to check local surveillance activities; and possibly to help the United Nations establish and maintain sensor lines and monitor all movements into and out of restricted areas. SFM-type assignments would apparently be feasible in Lebanon and on the Golan.

At present, American civilians conduct tactical early warning in Sinai. They detect by monitoring movements into, or preparations to move into, the Giddi and Mitla Passes; and verify access to the Egyptian and Israeli surveillance stations.[33] Although the SFM has the reputation of 'managing-out suspicions and negotiating confidence', future operations at the Passes or elsewhere in Sinai, on the Golan or on the Israeli–Lebanese border would depend on the agreement of the local parties. They would have to decide whose presence was politically acceptable and agree on suitable locations.

As for local party attitudes, the omens are good in Israel.[34] But for the Egyptians and Syrians, what matters is sovereignty. It is not so much the idea of third party early warning stations which concerns them – if these added to their security, then their location would be negotiable. More important would be questions relating to the kind of early warning station and its manning. Who would do the monitoring? Some options can be discarded. The idea of joint local teams performing the task is plainly years away. Not only would mutual confidence be lacking, but certainly the Syrians would not accept the Israelis in this role.[35] Remotely-controlled equipment has to be ruled out, too, because without people to do the checking, there could be false alerts and catastrophic mistakes. In any case, equipment costs would be prohibitive: and the essential element, at least for Israel, of the human 'trip-wire' would be missing.

In a final settlement, Israel will want to involve the Americans, if only as civilians, in the supervision of early warning safeguards. As in the 1975 Sinai Interim Agreement, an American presence would be seen as a tangible commitment to Israel's security – an obviously stronger deterrent than UN operations. Syria has traditionally been opposed to the presence of foreign powers on its sovereign territory, but if it, or any other Arab state, wanted the Soviets present with the Americans, an equal number of Soviet civilians should not create a problem, even apparently for the Israelis.[36]

To sum up, it might be possible for the Americans alone to continue monitoring operations in Sinai in a final settlement. But, if new monitoring stations are to be established on other fronts, the Russians – who insist on parity with the Americans – would wish to participate on an equal basis with them.[37] Whether the monitoring is carried out by separate Super Power monitoring teams (with or without the help of Britain and France) or by the Super Powers and others as UN observers would not much matter. The important requirement would be that information should be made available to all local parties and to the United Nations.

iv) Local party air reconnaissance supplements intelligence gathered from local surveillance stations and from UN sources. Apart from providing early warning, high definition aerial photography helps to confirm that local parties are keeping to agreements. Though local surveillance flights were only informal under the 1974 Sinai Disengagement Agreement, they became institutionalised in 1975. Since aerial photography can be used to back up complaints, it is useful to UN inspectors too. Indeed, the latter are required to 'carry out additional inspections within twenty-four hours' if requested by either party, and must 'promptly furnish' both parties with inspection results.[38] Furthermore, there could be added reassurance if local party overflights were extended to the full areas to be demilitarised and over any LFAs created.[39] Another valuable innovation, suggested by a former State Department official, would be a 'joint photo-interpretation' team to discuss data collected.[40]

v) American aerial reconnaissance (Soviet MiG-25 reconnaissance is assumed to take place), established with the 1975 Sinai Interim Agreement, is a key verification measure, not least because results of American missions (every seven to ten days) provide Israel, Egypt and the United Nations with additional surveillance data. But formalised Soviet air reconnaissance of buffer zones (as opposed to satellite reconnaissance, which presumably takes place anyway) should be part of a final agreement: it might provide a welcome second source of information for all parties, particularly the Syrians.

The need for improvements outlined in this section will be crucial if the United Nations is to act as an efficient early warning safeguard on Israel's frontiers with Egypt and Syria. However, because the United Nations is unlikely to be able to act as a combat force, an alternative method is discussed in the next section to fulfil the guarantor tasks required on Israeli and Jordanian frontiers with a new Palestinian entity and on the Israeli–Lebanese frontier.

If international guarantor forces for West Bank and Gaza frontiers and the Israeli–Lebanese frontier are to be efficient, they will have to overcome similar and even greater difficulties than those affecting UN peace-keeping forces when it comes to their mandate, command structure and composition. However, like the

UN peace-keeping forces on other frontiers, guarantor forces on the Lebanese, West Bank and Gaza Strip frontiers would require the symbolic support of the Super Powers acting in a monitoring capacity. Similarly, the guarantor forces would be heavily dependent on most of the verification techniques and possible improvements described above: border surveillance; ground and air surveillance by outside parties, including American and Soviet representatives; and local party air reconnaissance (in these cases, Israeli and Jordanian, and Israeli and Lebanese, and possibly Syrian).

II THE WEST BANK AND GAZA STRIP

1. Political and Security Requirements

Central to the Arab–Israeli dispute is the Palestinian question. Without a solution to this, there can be no comprehensive settlement. To find common ground on which a Palestinian solution could be based, minimum Israeli and Palestinian demands (which may change) must be taken into account. Many Israelis regard the West Bank and Gaza Strip as their own land by biblical right, or as land crucial to their security and over which, therefore, Israel must maintain military control. This runs directly counter to the minimum Palestinian demand for the right to self-determination and for an independent state on the West Bank and Gaza Strip.

Any Israeli government confronted by the prospect that one day a Palestinian entity might not be under its own military control would be likely to make two basic demands: i) that the area of the West Bank and Gaza Strip from which Israel might eventually withdraw should be demilitarised (with no arms except those required for a Palestinian internal police force) unless and until Israel, Jordan and the new entity's political authority decided otherwise: and, ii) that demilitarisation and its maintenance should be as effective and as long-lasting as any present or future Israeli military control, or as the Allon, Dayan and Begin Plans might have been. The chief threats against which Israelis say they would need protection are: terrorist raids; the risk that the West

Bank would become a Soviet base; and the infiltration of arms, particularly artillery pieces, into the West Bank.

Although there may be differences between the positions of the PLO and some West Bank Palestinians, there are likely to be two minimum Palestinian demands: i) a prompt and complete Israeli evacuation to enable Palestinians to assume complete self-government as quickly as possible; and, ii) the provision of physical international guarantees (other than from Arab states) against Israeli or Arab armed incursions. The Palestinians would want protection from Israeli reprisal raids, which may be induced by accident, and from conventional attack (Israeli or Arab), and possibly from infiltration of extremists seeking to upset internal stability.

The chief points of controversy arising from these demands are: first, how quickly should Palestinians assume political authority, regardless of whether this takes the form of limited autonomy or self-determination? Second, what type of security régime could cope with the different vulnerabilities of Israel and the Palestinians and how would it be implemented over time?

Military control of the West Bank is crucial to Israel's security; but that does not mean that Israel itself needs to exercise this control. It could be done by other means. If, therefore, the question of security guarantees could be arranged by other means and to the satisfaction of both Israel and the Palestinians, this could produce the political solution to their conflicting demands.

2. Future Demilitarisation

There is now broad international consensus that a Palestinian entity on the West Bank and Gaza Strip (linked by a corridor) will have to be virtually demilitarised, whatever its future constitutional arrangements;[41] and that token strips of Israeli and Jordanian territory should also be demilitarised. It seems possible that many Palestinians and even the PLO would accept a severe limit on the militarisation of their new entity. Whilst the PLO publicly rejects the limit on sovereignty that demilitarisation implies, two members of Fatah's Central Committee have privately indicated that the PLO would not necessarily reject outright some form of 'limitation of armaments'.[42] Furthermore, the PLO recognises that the Palestinians could not rely on self-defence and would need to depend on non-Arab external forces to protect their territory from Israeli re-occupation or Arab intervention.[43]

As for their Soviet supporters, Soviet academics see no difficulty in maintaining what would amount to the demilitarised status of Palestinian territory, provided the Palestinians agree. In addition, many Middle East analysts consider that with a satisfactory settlement on the Golan, it is not inconceivable that Syria might lean on the Palestinians to accept this limit on their sovereignty. It seems, therefore, that, with the exception of a lightly-armed security force to maintain internal order, demilitarisation of their territory may be the price that Palestinians are prepared and obliged to pay in return for territory and for outside protection.

However, the Palestinians will not willingly accept the loss of sovereignty that limitation of armaments and international military control entails. In compensation, it can be argued, they should be given the fullest degree of self-government as quickly as possible over all the West Bank and Gaza Strip, and they should regain their part of Jersualem. This would mean that the Palestinians should at least be given the choice (regardless of how far they are influenced in this by neighbouring Arab states)[44] to decide on their political future. They may or may not decide to federate with Jordan. This would not matter so long as Palestinian territory is demilitarised to the extent described. The aim would be to satisfy the aspirations of the majority of Palestinians, thereby preventing Rejectionists from gaining support for irredentist claims on Israel during or after implementation of the settlement.[45]

Nevertheless, Israel, which is, in any case, adamantly opposed to an independent state, would be wary of Palestinian offers on arms limitations. Regarding the security threat that an independent Palestinian state would pose to Israel, a former Israeli diplomat has said: 'Our fear about the West Bank becoming a sovereign state, with or without the Gaza Strip, is not fear of the Arabs ... but fear of the Russians. ... Whatever demilitarisation provisions the Palestinians might be willing to accept to gain their independence, once they're independent there would be nothing to stop them inviting the Russians in ... the state would become a Soviet bastion'.[46] Israeli anxieties will not, therefore, have been allayed by the PLO's public statement that an independent state would not be 'a Soviet military base and would not seek to supply itself with modern systems of missiles'.[47]

Since the Israeli Government understandably will not be convinced by Palestinian statements concerning limitation of arms and since the Palestinians recognise that they themselves could not defend their own territory, the firm and indefinite military guarantees that both Israelis and Palestinians need must be provided by the international community.

The essential requirement, therefore, is to devise a combination of demilitarisation and international guarantees which are sufficiently convincing to persuade Israel that a Palestinian 'homeland' would not threaten Israel's security. Likewise, security measures should reassure Palestinians that neither Israel nor Arab states could intervene in Palestinian territory. The crucial questions are: first, who would perform the necessary enforcement tasks, and second, how might this be done?

3. Enforcement:

A. Evolutionary Plan

One approach is that advocated by a number of American academics and which is apparently close to the State Department's own line of thinking.

First, they assume that neither Israel nor Arab states could sell overnight the idea of full withdrawal or full peace to their respective publics. They therefore conclude that implementation of a settlement would have to be gradual and allow for concessions by Israelis and Palestinians.[48] This would permit psychological adjustment. Second, they express a preference in adopting known security arrangements such as Sinai-type early warning safeguards and traditional UN peace-keeping methods for the West Bank and Gaza Strip.

For the purposes of analysis, political and security arguments need to be separated. According to this scheme, political concessions might be as follows: i) a full withdrawal of Israeli administration, which should be replaced by an international transitional authority (ITA)[49] working with a Palestinian authority until Constituent Assembly elections; or by a joint administration of Israeli, Jordanian and Palestinian representatives (as foreseen by Begin) during a transitional phase; ii)

103

Israel would surrender claims to political sovereignty on the West Bank and Gaza Strip; the Palestinians would surrender the idea of total independence and accept federation with Jordan.

It is argued that such a political plan would facilitate the implementation of demilitarisation provisions and a Sinai-type security régime: i) the West Bank and Gaza Strip would be the demilitarised zone of Jordan; but the Palestinians would, in partial compensation, have their own lightly-armed security force; ii) there would be a phased withdrawal of the IDF in exchange for steps towards peace: but the presence of the IDF would be non-offensive and temporary, intended to safeguard Israel during the period of re-adjustment.

The approach has obvious attractions. First, if a Palestinian entity took the form of a demilitarised autonomous unit federated to Jordan, this would separate the Israeli and Jordanian military forces. A degree of early warning (time and space) would have been achieved for both these countries. Second, the responsibility for keeping the area demilitarised would be shared between the IDF with military outposts on the West Bank and Jordanian troops who would patrol the Jordan River, supposedly to prevent arms infiltration. A hope that Palestinian terrorism could be thus prevented is expected to put a stop to Israeli reprisal raids and to deter an Israeli re-occupation of the West Bank. Such a scheme would thereby relieve potential external guarantors of any direct responsibility for violations of a demilitarised Palestinian entity. Third, the longer the IDF stayed, it was maintained in Washington, the less would be asked of the UN peace-keeping force around a Palestinian entity.[50] Such a force would only need to participate in inspection, provide the familiar 'plate glass window' and serve as a moral deterrent. Fourth, the Jordan River would be Israel's chief security frontier, permitting the open borders that Israel seeks on the Israeli–Palestinian frontier.

But this approach carries enormous weaknesses. The Israelis would not be likely to trust Jordanian troops (many of whom must be Palestinians) to enforce demilitarisation on the West Bank; nor, with its deep scepticism of UN peace-keeping forces, would Israel ever wish to depend on them in any degree in so sensitive an area as the West Bank. Israel would, therefore, surely reserve the right (along the lines of the 1974 Israel–Syria Disengagement Agreement) to retaliate against any suspicion of terrorists using

Palestinian territory as a base.[51] This could upset the peace settlement as a whole.

Second, this American approach would offer no protection to the inhabitants of the West Bank and Gaza Strip against Israeli incursions: a UN peace-keeping force, inevitably operating under Chapter VI of the UN Charter, would be unlikely to have a mandate or be sufficiently equipped to stop massive Israeli reprisal raids, and unarmed Palestinians could not defend themselves.

Third, if the Palestinians are to be asked to accept virtual demilitarisation indefinitely, they should not in addition be expected to accept an indefinite Israeli military presence and an enforced federation with Amman. Under these circumstances, Palestinian Rejectionists could be expected to flourish and gain support – which might lead to an extremist leadership on the West Bank and might threaten Amman's moderate régime with overthrow.

Finally, the success of this American approach assumes the continuation of political stability of all neighbouring Arab régimes and their willingness to continue to perform a policing role along the Jordan River of a peace settlement that many Arabs certainly would not approve – because of what would be likely to be the indefinitely protracted presence of the Israeli army.

B. *Innovatory Security Plan*

The above approach clearly leaves a large credibility gap. It resembles the Begin Plan too closely and does not offer sufficient assurance that the near to demilitarised status of a Palestinian entity would be guaranteed, except by action of the IDF. After talks with military and political experts, it is possible to advocate a second approach that would take account of the above weaknesses.

The approach is based on an acceptance of the fact that both Super Powers are present in the area (see Chapters 3 and 4). It also takes account of a procedural constraint: since Palestinian sovereignty will be circumscribed by virtue of limits on armaments, the Palestinians should not be asked to accept the one condition that most of them would refuse – a continual Israeli presence on their soil. Moreover, a gradual withdrawal, it is

105

argued, would encourage those on *either* side who wanted to sabotage peace.[52]

If, therefore, the Palestinians are to accept a militarily-truncated 'homeland', they should be permitted to set up their own transitional Palestinian régime, which would assume immediate political authority when Israel withdrew. The problem of which group of Palestinians to hand over to would have been decided at Geneva, or an alternative conference centre. It would then be for the Palestinian régime to decide whether it wanted international help in its administrative tasks and whether the Arab League, United Nations or Four Powers might provide it.[53] After Constituent Assembly elections, a new Palestinian government could choose whether or not to federate with Jordan.

i) Border Guard

Since the Palestinians would only have a lightly-armed security force – to be called the Palestinian Army – the West Bank and Gaza Strip would be defenceless. Similarly, if Israel is to withdraw its military presence in a single step, and to refrain from retaliating against guerrilla raids across an Israeli–Palestinian frontier, then it, too, must be properly protected. Thus, the requirement would be for an international guarantor force (Border Guard) stationed astride the Israeli–Palestinian frontier and along the Jordan River, regardless of the constitutional relationship with Jordan.

The crucial tasks of the Border Guard on the West Bank and Gaza Strip (and along the connecting corridor between them) would be: to maintain the demilitarised status of or limitations of armaments in those areas and in token strips of Israel and Jordan by a) denying access to Israeli and Arab forces, b) preventing terrorist raids and reprisals across Palestinian frontiers, c) sealing Palestinian frontiers against the entry of illegal arms, and, d) confiscating those that escaped detection at the frontier. It should also protect farmers working in border areas. To fulfil these tasks, the force would need a strong mandate and the full political backing of contributing powers.

The relationship of the Border Guard and the Palestinian internal security force would inevitably be sensitive. To facilitate the task of excluding illegal arms and of ensuring respect for a ban on para-military training, the Border Guard and Palestinian

106

security force should cooperate in investigating alleged breaches of the peace agreements on Palestinian territory. But if the Palestinian authorities wished to reduce their involvement, then the Border Guard would carry out the necessary inspection on its own. If breaches were discovered, the Border Guard (or, alternatively, a special force set up for this purpose only) would be empowered to apprehend and disarm the offenders. However, Palestinians would insist that their own civil administration be respected. Therefore, in order to preserve good relations with the Palestinian authorities, those apprehended would be handed over to their respective political authority, after being disarmed.

Any Israeli offenders against the Peace Treaty provisions who were caught by the Border Guard in the DMZs would be handed back to their national authorities.

Apart from Israel's strong objection to being made dependent on a body it regards as being both ineffectual and prejudiced, it is unlikely that the United Nations would undertake these tasks. Theoretically, that body can use force to maintain or restore international peace and security. But although the United Nations has authorised the use of force (other than in self-defence) under the special circumstances of the Congo, the effect of that procedure has been to generate a strong objection amongst most member states to a repetition. Certainly there would be objections to creating a force with sufficient capacity to police the borders of a new Palestinian entity. Some member states would see this as discrimination against the Palestinians and would shy away from the unenviable task with its inevitable political kick-back; other member states, taking an Israeli point of view, would be sceptical of the United Nations' willingness to fight or to act impartially. In any case, Israel is unlikely to agree to depend on a UN force.

Besides these political difficulties, there would be practical objections. First, the requirement for a balanced and impartial UN force, capable of effective operation and prepared to suffer a high rate of casualties, would be difficult to meet. Not only would contributing states have to be prepared to commit troops for longer periods, but they would have to do so in the sure knowledge that such troops would be expected to engage in combat to prevent terrorism and reprisal raids.[54] Second, there would be the problem of referring to the Security Council for particular military actions and the delays that this would incur.

Whether the Security Council could renew the mandate of an international force against strong local opposition has been regarded as doubtful in the past and has not been considered as a serious option by UN officials with experience of other situations.[55] But in the case of the West Bank and Gaza Strip and all the security problems that these particular territories would present, the duration of the UN mandate would have to be of a different order – entailing an indefinite commitment by the Security Council (in effect, by the Super Powers) to stability on those frontiers. This is not inconceivable. The UN has remained for fifteen years in Cyprus. And objections to longer mandates in the past have been based on the argument that UN forces are emergency forces located on Egyptian and Syrian sovereign territory. But the West Bank and Gaza Strip would present a novel situation: if the Palestinian 'homeland', or state, had come into being on condition that an international force was stationed on its borders for, say, fifteen years, the sovereignty issue would not apply. Here, the initial mandate could be for fifteen years, after which there would be a review of how to *improve* the operation of the force. Israelis, Jordanians and Palestinians could then rest assured that the force would not be withdrawn until they agreed that it should. Whether a majority of the member states of the United Nations could agree to such an indefinite undertaking, which would in any case require more member states to be prepared to undertake peace-keeping tasks, is doubtful.

ii) Middle East Control Commission

Could, therefore, a Border Guard be set up outside UN auspices? An inter-governmental organisation could be created under an eventual Middle East Peace Treaty, registered with the United Nations. Its constitutional status would be like that of other treaty organisations. Possibly based in Geneva, a Control Commission could authorise, recruit and administer a Border Guard which would have the mandate to police Palestinian frontiers and fight, if necessary, to repel minor interventions across them.

The Control Commission would consist of Treaty signatories, the Super Powers (as Co-Chairmen), West and East European states, and any other states prepared to support a Middle East peace settlement and resulting agreements. The aim would be a politically-balanced representation, and all members would have to be approved by Israel and its neighbours, as well as by the United States and the Soviet Union. The Commission would have a Secretary General and Secretariat.

The Control Commission would be financed by its members according to their means: it might also be supported by the oil-producing states and oil-using states (e.g. Japan) which profit from peace in the Middle East.

iii) Form and Composition of Border Guard

As for the form and composition of the guarantor force, the Secretary General, military and civil staff and national contingents would come under the Control Commission's authority. National contingents could not come from i) any Middle Eastern states; ii) the United States or Soviet Union; or, iii) from states unacceptable to Israel, Jordan or a Palestinian entity. However, there would have to be an 'equitable geographic representation', a concept formalised with UNEF II, requiring equal contributions from NATO and the Warsaw Pact, as well as a representation of non-aligned states. The Force Commander would come from a non-aligned state.

National contingents would need to be i) militarily qualified to fulfil the tasks discussed above, and, ii) recruited from states which would be politically willing for their contingents to engage in combat and suffer casualties and which would be prepared to commit troops for a specified period of time.[56]

iv) Mandate

These requirements, crucial to the effectiveness of the Border Guard in this fragile situation, would need to be set out in a clearly-stated mandate. The chief points would be:

a) that the Control Commission provide the Secretary General with the authority to issue directives to the Force Commander to enforce strict control of the West Bank and Gaza Strip frontiers;

b) that the contributing states be formally committed to the enforcement function of the Border Guard so that they could not readily withdraw their contingents.

Israel will have deep anxieties about withdrawing from the West Bank, forfeiting its military supervision and accepting the creation of a Palestinian entity. Similarly, Palestinians will fear the proximity of Israel (and some Palestinians would say they need guarantees not only against Israel, but also against their Arab neighbours). In addition, neither Israelis nor Palestinians would want to accept guarantees that were not permanent because of the fear that changes in the other's government might undermine the political settlement. International military control would therefore have to be as permanent as possible, preferably indefinite. The duration of the mandate of the guarantor force could not be limited or qualified. While there could be no such thing as a permanent Border Guard, the challenge is to create one with as long a life as possible.

One way of ensuring this would be to make the stationing of the Border Guard a condition of Palestinian self-determination, as would be the virtual demilitarisation of the West Bank and Gaza Strip. At first, such a force might be set up under a Middle East Peace Treaty with control over all demilitarised Palestinian territory. After Constituent Assembly elections, the force would withdraw to the border areas where it would have jurisdiction over frontier strips. In the final analysis, the permanency of the Border Guard would depend on the political interest of the Super Powers in keeping it there. If they were to withdraw their support, this would signal the onset of instability. It follows, therefore, that such a force is likely to be as permanent and as effective as the Super Powers want it to be. However, once constituted, it would be hard for either Super Power to withdraw from the support of this force without leaving it under the protection of the other Super Power alone.

v) Location and Technical Feasibility

To fulfil the tasks described above, the Border Guard would be stationed around the Israeli–Palestinian border (West Bank and Gaza Strip) and along the Jordan River. It would need to have jurisdiction (but not sovereignty) in demilitarised buffer strips of five hundred metres wide on each side of the border; the strips would be of equal size in Israel, the Palestinian entity and Jordan, and would be clearly demarcated by sensor lines. Each party would cede irreversibly to the Control Commission the right to use the frontier strips and to control access to any air-strip needed by the Border Guard outside them. However, in practice, it would be impossible to maintain a presence on the land of an antagonistic local party. In this case, the width proposed above would permit operations to continue from one side of the frontier only, if one national party withdrew its cooperation.

The technical feasibility of such operations is not in doubt. Military experts suggest that the force should consist of infantry armed with light missiles, armoured personnel carriers (APCs), heavy mortars and have air support. The Border Guard could be logistically maintained from Cyprus. If an air-field there (possibly the RAF base at Akrotiri) was made available, large aircraft could bring in supplies and reinforcements. Thereafter, transport by light aircraft to air-strips in the frontier zones would be adequate for servicing.[57] Sufficient financing and supplies would need to be made available and Control Commission members should, therefore, help by earmarking manpower and logistical support for the use of the Border Guard.[58]

The size of the force necessary to operate efficiently and economically would depend on equipment and on whether minor border rectifications could be agreed to improve the line of sight for monitoring movements across the borders. But with the most up-to-date equipment, a force to prevent raids across these frontiers need not be of great size: estimates vary between five thousand and ten thousand men. And, in any event, the Border Guard would not be intended to engage in full-scale battle. Under present circumstances, there is little threat of a surprise attack being launched against Israel on this eastern front.[59]

vi) Surveillance

An efficient and impartial surveillance system to monitor and verify military activities around the Israeli–Palestinian border and along the Jordan River would be crucial to effective Border Guard operations, and therefore to any settlement that Israelis, Palestinians and Jordanians could accept. This is because i) the military credibility and reliability of the Border Guard and its linked monitoring system would be a key factor in persuading the Israelis to withdraw; and, ii) the Palestinians would need to be

111

assured that Israeli intervention in their territory was detected and prevented. Therefore, as in the case of demilitarisation provisions and the stationing of the Border Guard itself, monitoring stations should be part of the *quid pro quo* for the establishment of a Palestinian entity and for the full peace Israel seeks. Nor could Israelis or Palestinians impose their preferences on the manning of the monitoring system. The system would come under the authority of the Control Commission and would consist of unmanned sensors, watch stations and on-site inspection teams set up astride Israeli–Palestinian borders and along the Jordan River.

The monitoring stations would ideally be located in the frontier strips themselves. If states contributing personnel to monitoring teams considered that this involved too high a degree of vulnerability, the monitoring stations could be located at less vulnerable positions by negotiation with the neighbouring authorities. They would then be linked to local watch stations, say at five-mile intervals, in the frontier strips. An essential requirement would be to have impartial observers at these read-out stations, for it would be on their interpretation of data that the Border Guard would take action. The Control Commission would have to ensure that monitoring and observer teams consisted of a balanced representation of Western, Communist, Third World and non-aligned countries belonging to the Control Commission.

Of fundamental importance, of course, would be the presence of American and Soviet personnel on this front. As on the other fronts, their role would be strictly non-combatant. They would be attached in a civilian capacity to the monitoring stations, but their personnel would not come under the Force Commander, nor could they instruct him except through the Control Commission. By participating in monitoring and by providing air recon-naissance data, as well as financial and logistic support, the Super Powers would demonstrate their identification with and commit-ment to the success of the Border Guard and the security régime on the West Bank and Gaza Strip. If Super Power civilians were located in more vulnerable positions in the frontier strips, this would add considerably to their vital symbolic deterrent effect.

vii) Open Borders

By contrast with the American approach outlined above where the

Jordan River would be Israel's main security line (at least for an interim period during which Israel maintained military control over the rest of the West Bank), there would under this second scheme be no open Israeli–Palestinian frontier. Instead, there would be electronic and unmanned sensors all along the meandering populated districts of Israel's frontiers with the West Bank and Gaza Strip. Consequently, there could only be a limited number of crossing-points on this frontier, as along the Jordan River. The drawback here is that these devices would be vulnerable to false alarms and this would necessitate more manpower for on-site inspection purposes. But, over time, the barriers could be lifted, but only as and when *both* parties agreed. Given the close economic ties between Israel and the West Bank and Gaza Strip, Israel and the Palestinians would want to remove the inconvenience of these security precautions as soon as their confidence in each other grew.

III JERUSALEM

Jerusalem poses other difficult security problems. As negotiations progress, compromise over the implementation of security measures should emerge. However, the basic pattern of West Bank and Gaza Strip security measures could be adopted here too: i) all Jerusalem could be demilitarised; ii) a Border Guard (supplied with the required proximity devices) could operate at sensitive points under the authority of the Control Commission; iii) Israel and the Palestinians could share civilian policing functions in the Holy Places; but, iv) should police separately those areas over which Israel and the new Palestinian entity respectively have administrative and political control.

IV THE LEBANON

1. Political and Security Requirements

Israeli and Lebanese political and security requirements will depend on whether a solution to the Palestinian question is found and on the speed of the Israeli administrative and military withdrawal from the West Bank. The longer the transitional period before the Palestinians are able to exercise fully their right of self-determination, the greater will be the sense of Palestinian frustration and the more likely that guerrilla incursions will escalate across the Israeli–Lebanese border. Israeli and Lebanese negotiating terms for final border arrangements have not been elaborated; but inevitably they must be linked to the key Palestinian issue.

While the Israelis have no claim to south Lebanon, they do regard the area south of the Litani as crucial to their border security. Israeli policy-makers will therefore need to be convinced that any security arrangements after a peace settlement will effectively deny the area to armed Palestinians. Until the UNIFIL experience, Israel had been unenthusiastic about the stationing of UN forces in Lebanon and had insisted that the Lebanese Government re-assert its own authority in the south.[60] But any Israeli government confronted by the prospect that it may not be able to carry out border patrols or provide military support for its Maronite Christian allies, would make two demands: that south Lebanon should become a buffer zone with all rival factions disarmed, and that it be effectively policed by the Lebanese Army and/or an international force; and, secondly, that the various factions remain disarmed indefinitely. In short, Israel would want guaranteed protection for its north Galileean villages.

For its part, Lebanon would require Israel not only to refrain from repeating its March 1978 intervention and carrying out reprisal raids, but also to cease its border patrols on Lebanese soil – an infringement of Lebanese sovereignty. In terms of security, the Lebanese Government has long considered the need for complete disarmament of rival factions, including the Palestinians, and has proposed the stationing of UN forces in south Lebanon.[61] Its acceptance of UNIFIL, prior to a peace settlement, revealed that it was not yet in a position to exercise its own authority over warring factions in the south. But, after a peace settlement, it would undoubtedly aim at least to assist any international force in its policing tasks.

Israel and Lebanon would be party to any international agreement concerning security measures on this frontier. But the presence of 300,000 Palestinian refugees (many of whom would not choose to settle in a new Palestinian entity) and of extremist

114

Palestinians rejecting a 'mini-state' solution would complicate the security tasks of Lebanese and international forces. For the Palestinians would have conflicting requirements: the Palestinian and Muslim Shiite civilians would demand protection from possible Israeli reprisals which may be provoked by accident or by guerrilla incursions into Israel; while the Palestinian extremists would demand the right to continue their armed struggle against Israel and would use the south Lebanese civilians as a convenient cover for their military activities.

The key points arising from these conflicting demands are: how quickly might the Palestinians assume political authority in their new entity? And, what type of security régime could cope with the different vulnerabilities of the Israelis and of the south Lebanese? Also, how might the security régime vary over time?

2. Buffer Zone

There is a broad consensus that all factions in the area south of the Litani River should be disarmed after a peace settlement; indeed, part of the tacit Red Line understanding was that the Syrians should help prevent guerrilla infiltration to the south.[62] Both the Lebanese and Syrians, fearful of being drawn into a wider Arab–Israeli confrontation, would favour an end to border raids and the directly-related Israeli reprisals that this disarming action would be intended to bring about; and civilians in the area would be spared from further Israeli punishment raids. But, as a reciprocal gesture, the Israelis would be expected to demilitarise a token strip on their side of the border.

It seems possible that the mainstream PLO would want to enforce the disarmament of their extremists if the Palestinians once had their 'homeland'. Guerrilla activity originating from the Lebanon would not only reflect unfavourably on the new Palestinian political authority, but also reinforce any Israeli attempts to sabotage the peace settlement. It is in this context that Yassir Arafat's effort to cooperate with UNIFIL and curb extremist military activities may be understood.

Although the Israelis have regarded Arafat's ability to cooperate with UNIFIL with interest, they are not likely to be convinced that this willingness to cooperate will continue or that it would be repeated either in south Lebanon or on the West Bank after a peace settlement. The essential requirement in the context of a settlement, therefore, is to devise security measures for south Lebanon that would prevent Palestinians from perpetrating raids across the border, and similarly reassure the south Lebanese that Israel could not intervene in Lebanese territory. Who would provide the necessary enforcement, and how?

3. Enforcement

Although UNIFIL's three-fold mandate has been clearly stated,[63] the complexity of its tasks has been demonstrated by the different demands of the Israelis and the PLO: the former require UNIFIL to deny south Lebanon to Palestinian guerrillas and to secure Israeli borders against fedayeen incursions; the latter stressed UNIFIL's purpose of confirming the withdrawal of Israeli forces, and have insisted that PLO cooperation with UNIFIL is not incompatible with the 1969 Cairo Agreement permitting the Palestinians to have a military sanctuary in south Lebanon.[64] What these conflicting requirements reveal is that an eventual defusion of Israeli–Palestinian tension on this border must lie in a solution to the Palestinian question. In the interim, they have focused attention on the need in south Lebanon for a UN force different in kind to, say, UNEF II (serving as a buffer force) and able to curb (by force, if necessary) infiltration of guerrillas or of unauthorised arms to the south; and able to deter a return of Israeli forces.

UNIFIL's task is complicated by a number of factors. The proximity of the Palestinian and Israeli populations is combined with terrain ideal for fedayeen activities. Then, also, the Lebanese Government is unlikely to be able to exercise 'effective authority' in the south for some time. Under these circumstances, a traditional UN peace-keeping force, serving mainly as an inter-position force, would not be able to guarantee the cessation of 'hostile activities' in the area that the Secretary General has called for. The south Lebanese would remain defenceless against renewed fedayeen–Israeli exchanges; and Israel's northern borders would be vulnerable to guerrilla raids. The well-known pattern of border raids and reprisals might re-assert itself. The challenge, the UN's biggest since the Congo operation eighteen years ago, has therefore been whether a UN force could bring peace and security to an area lacking effective government.

UNIFIL has attempted to cross this threshold. Militarily, its mandate amounts to creating a cordon sanitaire across south Lebanon – preventing Palestinians from attacking Israel and Israel from making retaliatory strikes against Lebanon. With its force of 6,000 men and with heavy equipment,[65] the UNIFIL operation has provided quasi-combatant conditions for a number of the world's armies; and so far no contributing state has withdrawn its contingent, despite casualties. Also, with active French participation, and with American, British and German logistic contributions, and with the backing of America as the sponsoring party, UNIFIL represents a symbolic deterrent.

An effective UNIFIL mission in the Lebanon would refute the long-held Israeli contention that no UN force could effectively perform anti-infiltration tasks. In so doing, it would provide a precedent for future UN peace-keeping tasks in Lebanon after a peace settlement, as well as on the borders of a Palestinian entity. But how high are the chances of success?

Until the Lebanese Government's authority has been restored in the south, UNIFIL alone would be expected to maintain law and order. Yet, by contrast with previous UN peace-keeping operations, no detailed agreements were worked out with the local parties before UNIFIL's units arrived. In short, there is no established authority on the Lebanese side with which Israel and the United Nations can deal. While it is too early to say how effective mainstream PLO members will be in policing their own Rejectionists, the fact is that for as long as UNIFIL operates within traditional UN peace-keeping guide-lines its success will depend on the ability and continued willingness of the PLO to cooperate with it. Once this fails, the danger of renewed fighting would be high. Militarily, UNIFIL is neither an offensive force nor equipped to match the heavily-armed Palestinians. At the political level, the high rate of casualties and the anti-PLO posture that UNIFIL would be forced to assume could encourage contributors to withdraw their contingents.[66] In short, an attack on UNIFIL would be an attack on the Security Council's peace-keeping methods and its ability to intervene in the settlement of disputes; and as yet there is no sign amongst UN officials or member states that the United Nations is ready to discard its neutral inter-position role between forces in favour of a full combatant role and the external administrative authority that this would require.

4. UNIFIL Precedent

As in the case of future policing tasks on the West Bank and Gaza Strip, there would be a built-in preference to adopt known UN peace-keeping safeguards in Lebanon after a final settlement. A UN force along traditional lines would have all the attractions spelt out in the previous section on the West Bank. First, the area south of the Litani would take the form of a buffer zone (demilitarised except for official Lebanese and international forces) and the Lebanese Government would be chiefly responsible for policing it (possibly helped by the Syrians north of the Litani River). If effective, this scheme would relieve potential external guarantors of responsibility for violations in the Lebanese buffer zone. Also, the more efficient the Lebanese Army became (and this would depend on the help it receives in its reconstruction and training), the less would be required of a UN peace-keeping force astride the Israeli–Lebanese border and in south Lebanon in terms of mandate, manpower, equipment and costs. Indeed, a UN force would carry out traditional inspection tasks and serve merely as an inter-position force.

But this approach carries the same striking weaknesses as would its counter-part on a Palestinian entity's borders. First, Israel would not trust the Lebanese Army, so recently split by sectarian fighting, to prevent hostilities in the south; its confidence in an international force, which, according to UN experts, might decide to withdraw if faced by full-blown Palestinian hostilities, would be low. So the Israelis would surely reserve the right to retaliate against any fedayeen incursions. Second, because a UN force would operate within traditional UN guide-lines, it would neither have the mandate nor be equipped to stop Israeli reprisals and the south Lebanese would once more be defenceless. This would mean that isolated incidents could escalate out of control – fuelling animosity between Israelis and Palestinians, possibly threatening to undermine other peace settlement agreements.

5. Border Guard Approach

The incentives for a UNIFIL success, so closely tied to American peace diplomacy, are high for Washington as well as the United

Nations. It is possible, therefore, that if UNIFIL were faced with potential failure in Lebanon, it might become a fighting force (with the tacit support of America) and cross the threshold from peace-keeping to peace-enforcing in order to fulfil its mission. Then the Border Guard-type force proposed for the West Bank would not be necessary. The United Nations would have, in effect, become an embryonic world government. Or, if the Lebanese Army could restore its authority in south Lebanon and be as effective as was the Jordanian Army in policing the Israeli–Jordanian border after 1953, there would be no need to consider the requirement for an international fighting force. But until these conditions are met, the requirement would be for a Border Guard guarantor force (outside UN auspices) stationed astride parts of the Israeli–Lebanese border and in the Palestinian-inhabited areas south of the Litani.

The crucial tasks of the Border Guard would be to ensure that south Lebanon remained free of fighting; to seal the area in the north along the Litani River and in the south along the border with Israel against the entry of illegal arms and to confiscate those escaping detection; to maintain demilitarisation of an Israeli token strip of territory; to prevent terrorist raids and reprisals across the Israeli–Lebanese border; and to carry out inshore patrols to prevent sea-borne raids.

6. Authority and Operational Principles

In all respects, the Border Guard in Lebanon would resemble its counter-part on the West Bank and Gaza Strip: it would come under the authority of the Middle East Control Commission; in terms of its form, composition and mandate, it would operate according to the same principles; and it would be logistically supplied from Akrotiri.

But there would be two important exceptions: i) if it was mutually decided between Israel and Lebanon that the Lebanese Army could effectively carry out the tasks required, the Border Guard would be simply replaced by a traditional UN peace-keeping force, possibly deployed in a narrow security belt astride the Israeli–Lebanese border; ii) if the Christians in their enclaves became an accepted element of the Lebanese Army, then the Border Guard might not be required to operate in the Christian areas bordering on Israel. This might enable the 'good fence' arrangements, to which the Israelis and south Lebanese attach so much importance in economic and humanitarian, as well as symbolic, terms, to continue.

Border Guard Versus UN: Advantages

The innovatory security plan proposed for the West Bank, Gaza Strip, Jerusalem and, possibly, Lebanon has a procedural drawback: the international community will be reluctant to create a new international security system to enforce demilitarisation provisions and a new inter-governmental organisation to manage this degree of military control, all outside the UN framework. But bureaucratic inertia and political difficulties should not prevent innovation when peace is at stake. By contrast, there are important advantages: i) a Border Guard with this strong mandate and with the power to apprehend would not be constrained by UN uncertainties or local party political variations; ii) Border Guard forces would meet the security needs of a Palestinian entity and its Israeli and Jordanian neighbours as well as of Lebanon in the north; iii) because the Border Guard would be empowered to prevent Israeli reprisal raids into Palestinian territory, the Soviet Union would be less likely to find itself in the embarrassing position of supporting a security system which did not protect its one-time clients; iv) although this would be a one-off operation, if it succeeded it could be repeated in other situations and might influence the development of the United Nations positively.

V. THE ROLE OF OUTSIDE PRESSURE

At this point, the discussion turns from the Lebanon and the West Bank and Gaza Strip (and the special guarantee arrangements that the frontiers of a Palestinian entity would require) to the difficult question of sanctions. The exercise of sanctions by the future external guarantors, in particular the Super Powers, would, of course, be the back-bone of border security arrangements on *all* fronts. Sufficient Super Power cooperation to permit enforcement of the settlement by diplomatic, economic and even military sanctions will be essential.

After a settlement, minor, perhaps accidental, violations of the agreements by both sides should be expected. Hopefully, as trust grows, the Joint Commissions in Sinai would deal with disputes arising from small incidents (along the lines of the former MACs). Similarly, international personnel working with a Palestinian or Jordanian internal security force would help resolve disputes in a new Palestinian entity.

However, it may be wise to assume that there will be more serious violations on all fronts: repeated infringements, terrorism and officially-supported reprisal raids. Major breaches of the settlement could include attempted re-militarisation in zones of limited or no forces or an attack on a UN post, say, in the Sinai, or on a Border Guard team on the West Bank; failure to cooperate with the United Nations and dispute resolution machinery; or failure to take action to control extremists raiding across borders. Early warning stations might even reveal preparations for an attack on any one of the frontiers. In such cases, Joint Commissions and national law procedures would be inapplicable.

1. United Nations

It has been suggested, therefore, that such violations could be referred to a neutral international body recognised by local parties as unbiased and set up under UN auspices. It would be responsible only for deciding who was the aggressor.[67] Such a body could act as no more than an umpire and even then could only do so in the event of blatant violations.

The question is, how strong will sanctions have to be if they are to stop violators, or deter violations from occurring in the first place? Assuming that diplomatic machinery had failed to prevent such violations,[68] what kind of action could be taken by the UN forces? On Israel's frontiers with Egypt and Syria, the DMZs and other safeguards would allow time, even in the event of surprise attack, for diplomacy to come into play and for the local parties to mobilise for self-defence. The Super Powers (and also Britain and France) could warn that as guarantors they intended to support the Peace Treaty by applying political and economic pressures. If this threat proved insufficient, either Super Power would supply military aid to its respective client if attacked (see pp. 122–123 for a discussion of the way the Super Powers might cooperate on this).

2. Multilateral Enforcement Procedures

Potential guarantors would undoubtedly prefer to act under UN auspices. But there might be disagreement within the United Nations over the degree of delegation of authority to the Secretary General. The Chinese would also be an unknown quantity. So, while no other body has the moral authority or experience of the United Nations, complementary arrangements outside it should be organised.

Those powers which would have given multilateral political guarantees (in a Declaration registered with the United Nations) of final borders could be expected to emphasise primary reliance on the DMZs and early warning safeguards to deter violations and conflict between the parties on Israel's frontiers with Egypt and Syria. But their political declaration should contain provision for the use of sanctions that they could implement independently of the United Nations if necessary.

In the case of the West Bank and the Israeli–Lebanese border, the international guarantor force would be authorised and equipped to prevent terrorism and reprisal raids, and capable of acting instantaneously against such incursions. If it failed to stop violations, then the Super Powers (or Four Powers and others) would work under the above multilateral political guarantee arrangements to impose certain sanctions aimed at restoring the *status quo ante*. What might these be?

3. Super Power Cooperation and 'Agreed Ground Rules'

The chief economic backers and military suppliers – the United States, the Soviet Union (and to a lesser extent, France and Britain) – would take the necessary action along previously agreed lines. Sanctions would be negative in form and would be limited to those that could be accomplished externally to the area and that did not require active Super Power cooperation on the spot.[69] Threats of delay or stoppages of economic aid to an aggressor, blockade of ships carrying goods to an aggressor or boycott of goods originating in such a state would all have an effect in the longer term, given the degree of dependence of Israel, Arab confrontation states and a future Palestinian entity on these four economic backers. However, since the Arab oil states could

122

provide an alternative source of aid to the Arab confrontation states, it would be important to enlist their support to help maintain the *status quo*. More seriously, the shipment of arms and spare parts permitted under the agreement could be stopped.[70] The implementation of sanctions would come close to being an automatic mechanism: it would depend on the single principle that the Super Powers could be expected to support their respective clients if these latter were threatened, but to desist from doing so if their clients sought to upset the *status quo*. If the Super Powers could not, or were unwilling to, cooperate to the degree necessary to implement such sanctions, it would mean a return to the uncertainties that have made the area so combustible in the past.

An essential pre-requisite (and this applies to guarantees of arms balances too – see page 147) would be an understanding by these economic backers and arms suppliers to cooperate in an emergency. Western diplomats in Moscow speculate that, once committed, the Soviets would be meticulous in observation of obligations.[71] If the signatory powers of the formal Declaration of guarantee failed to agree on a joint course of action, it is crucial that each guarantor should be prepared to carry out its obligations under the Declaration according to its interpretation, but within the 'agreed ground rules'. These would represent a formalisation of the present *de facto* understandings between the Super Powers to show restraint in their unilateral action and in their efforts to maintain a balance of forces between the confrontation states. The aim would be to prevent confrontation between the Super Powers and to preclude the possibility of unilateral military intervention. Any unilateral action taken that did not conform with the 'agreed ground rules' would signal a serious breach of Super Power understanding regarding their support of a settlement and would threaten future stability in this area. It would be at this point, if Israel's ultimate security was at stake, for example, that an American guarantee of last resort for Israel might be invoked. Then, similar *de facto*, if not formal, guarantees of some Arab states by the Soviet Union could be expected to come into play.[72] But the Palestinian entity might be an exception: its ultimate survival might depend on an agreement reached by the Super Powers to respect its non-aligned status.

123

[1] The Brookings Institution, *Toward Peace in the Middle East*, Washington, December 1975, p. 13.

[2] President Carter's statement at Aswan has further clarified the American position on the Palestinians: 'There must be a resolution of the Palestinian problem in all its aspects . . . it must recognise the legitimate rights of the Palestinian people and enable the Palestinians to participate in the determination of their own future'. *The Department of State News Release*, 4 January 1978.

[3] *USIS*, 10 March 1977. In an attempt to reconcile the Arab and Israeli positions, President Carter now favours an interim plan of five years for the West Bank and Gaza Strip, at the end of which Israeli military government would cease. *International Herald Tribune*, 16 January 1978.

[4] President Brezhnev's speech to the 16th Congress of Soviet Trade Unions, 21 March 1977.

[5] One product of the October War and of Kissinger's diplomacy has been the wider understanding of the importance of DMZs and of peace-keeping forces as safeguards: Article V of the 1975 Sinai Interim Agreement states that UNEF is 'essential' to the parties. Thus, a precedent has been created for formal DMZs, and limitations of ground forces and weapons in certain areas. Under the Sinai Interim Agreement, 75 tanks, 72 artillery pieces and 8,000 troops are permitted in the limited-forces-and-armaments zones (LFAs).

[6] World Service News Bulletin, 13 January 1978.

[7] President Assad, like President Sadat, has accepted to negotiate DMZs once peace is established – on two conditions: that they be limited and that they be on each side of the border. *Financial Times* (London), 6 May 1977.

[8] *Financial Times* (London), 12 January 1978; *Financial Times* (London), 16 January 1978; President Sadat's interview with *October Magazine*, 15 January 1978. For a discussion of the Rafiah area, see Appendix I.

[9] *International Herald Tribune*, 12 January 1978; *International Herald Tribune*, 13 January 1978; Yehonathan Tommer, 'Mr. Begin's Peace Plan: The Domestic Reaction', *The World Today*, Vol. 34, No. 3, March 1978, p. 78.

[10] The US is working with Begin's proposal for the West Bank and trying to pin down its practical meaning in ways to ease Arab fears. *International Herald Tribune*, 19 May 1978.

[11] It has been suggested that the DMZ should be at least twice as wide as the range of SAMs, because either side may feel secure in venturing to the forward edge of SAM coverage before becoming really vulnerable. Therefore, to increase the hazards of engagement and thereby reduce the risk of conflict, the DMZ should be 60 kilometres wide – twice the range of the present generation of SAMs.

[12] For a discussion of the Rafiah area, see Appendix I.

[13] The 1975 Sinai Interim Agreement permitted Egypt to re-occupy some of the area (albeit with only limited forces) from which the IDF withdrew. This meant that Israel had given up what it regarded as a sacred negotiating principle – that all territory relinquished should be demilitarised. The UN buffer zone created was, therefore, smaller than it might have been. Although Israel retained a large buffer zone of its own in Sinai, some saw this as a 'dangerous precedent' for Israel and for possible future agreements where the size of demilitarisation would be vital to Israel's security. See Matti Golan, *The Secret Conversations of Henry Kissinger*, Bantam Books, 1976, p. 250.

[14] Although Israeli diplomats argue that there is no room on Israeli sovereign

124

territory for DMZs, precedents do exist: at the time of the 1949 armistice agreements, Israel evacuated areas west of the old international frontiers which were then demilitarised, together with the Israeli populated settlements of Ein Gev and Dardara. Israel regarded these as part of its sovereign territory, although Syria objected that they came within the competence of the Mixed Armistice Commission (MAC). Similarly, El Auja, part of the Latrun no-man's-land and the Jewish sector of the Mount Scopus enclave, all on the Israeli side of the international frontiers, were demilitarised under the armistice agreements. Nor are these isolated examples of Israeli acceptance. Part of the Israeli area of limited forces and armaments agreed in the 1974 Israel–Syria Disengagement Agreement covers Israeli territory west of the old international frontier. See Michael Comay, 'U.N. Peace-Keeping in the Israel–Arab Conflict, 1948–75: An Israel Critique', *Jerusalem Papers on Peace Problems*, No. 17–18, 1976, for a discussion of demilitarised and restricted zones. Note also the argument of an Israeli professor, who says that, to be effective, an agreement on demilitarisation should be based on the principles of reciprocity, relativity and free consent. It is futile to create security on one side of the frontier if apprehension and mistrust exist on the other. In delimiting the zone and formulating its régime, account should be taken of the relative circumstances of a geographical, strategic, political or ethnic nature, with a view to avoiding inequality of treatment. See N. Bar Yaacov, *The Israeli–Syrian Armistice: Problems of Implementation, 1949–1966*, Jerusalem, Magnes Press, Hebrew University, 1967, pp. 319f, 286, 337. Cited in Malcolm H. Kerr (Ed.), *The Elusive Peace in the Middle East*, State University of New York Press, Albany, 1975, pp. 93, 101, n. 86.

[15] From the 1967 Israeli–Syrian border, it is only 70 kilometres to Damascus.

[16] Interview data.

[17] Ian M. F. Smart, 'Military Insecurity and the Arab–Israel Conflict: There is an effective alternative to the United Nations', *New Middle East*, No. 26, November 1970, p. 30.

[18] For a discussion of current tasks of UN forces in the Middle East, see James O. C. Jonah, 'Peacekeeping in the Middle East', *International Journal*, Canadian Institute of International Affairs, Winter Issue, 1975/6.

[19] Disengagement Agreement between Israeli and Syrian Forces of 31 May 1974, and Protocol. Interview data.

[20] The efficiency of the command structure might partly depend on the eventual findings of the UN Committee of 33 drawing up guide-lines on 'specific questions' relating to peace-keeping. United Nations document A/AC. 121/L.27 and Appendix I, 4 November 1976.

[21] Force Commanders might have political advisers on their own staffs.

[22] The SRSG would have legal advisers. He would liaise with Force Commanders and the Chief Coordinator over economic and political aspects of military operations and would seek to find resolutions to local disputes.

[23] See N. A. Pelcovits, 'UN Peacekeeping and the 1973 Arab–Israeli Conflict', *Orbis*, Spring 1975, p. 165.

[24] Note however that UNEF I stayed for 11 years and the UN Force in Cyprus (UNFICYP) for 14 years and is still there. Although in 1970 Secretary Rogers foresaw a force of a 'continuing nature' in the Middle East, the present US Administration speaks cautiously of time periods. The Soviets are no more explicit: DMZs will last for some 'clearly specified period of time'. President Brezhnev's

speech to the 16th Congress of Soviet Trade Unions, 21 March 1977.

(25) Long-term mandates are not new. The mandates of the UN force in the Congo and of UNEF I were unlimited. Future long-term mandates will require as firm a commitment as constitutionally possible from member states to provide necessary financing.

(26) At each renewal of UNEF, Britain has indicated it would expect to participate in any guarantee force set up in a final settlement. But defence experts argue that a British contingent could only be provided at the expense of other commitments, particularly to NATO. France, too, has suggested that there could be contingents from Security Council members. See interview with the French Foreign Minister, *The Middle East*, July 1977. Also interview data.

(27) In a statement issued by the European Council meeting in London on 29 June 1977, the Nine for the first time collectively offered to 'consider participating in guarantees in the framework of the United Nations'. However, it is unlikely that the Danes or Dutch would supply contingents.

(28) Interview data.

(29) See the joint American–Soviet statement of 1 October 1977 on the principles and objectives to govern a re-convened Geneva Conference. *The Times* (London), 3 October 1977. Also interview data.

(30) Interview data. And for a similar conclusion, see N. A. Pelcovits, 'Security Guarantees in a Middle East Settlement', Foreign Policy Research Institute, *Sage Publications*, 1976, p. 49.

(31) Interview data. See also, ibid., p. 50.

(32) The past record of UN prevention of terrorist raids in populated areas has been poor. In 1972, the Chief of Staff, UNTSO, admitted that observers on the Lebanese side of the border could serve no practical function in this respect. See Comay, op. cit., p. 61.

(33) A self-developed task, in support of these functions, has been detecting Bedouin known to wander through the Wadi of Eight Wells near Giddi.

(34) In response to a question on the stationing of technicians on the Golan, former Israeli Defence Minister, Shimon Peres, has said: 'I do not reject this'. Jerusalem Domestic Television Service in Hebrew, 2 February 1977. Former Israeli Chief of Staff Mordechai Gur has commented that a Sinai-type agreement could be applied to any frontier – including the Golan. *Jerusalem Post International Edition*, 18 January 1977.

(35) The principle of mingling local party civilians with monitoring teams should be considered for the future. Though unacceptable at first, such a joint presence later on could inculcate the habit of cooperation.

(36) Although an American civilian presence on all fronts, including possibly at Sharm-el-Shaikh, is the preferred Israeli option, senior Israeli diplomats have not ruled out a Soviet civilian role in a settlement. As one of them said: 'We always thought the Soviets must have a role – once they normalise, they could play a more positive role as a politically moderating force ... they could play a civilian role'. Interview data. Although he discards the idea of the Super Powers as peace-keepers, Comay (op. cit., p. 51) also concedes the situation might change with a settlement and a resumption of diplomatic relations with Israel. A Super Power peace-keeping role might then have more appeal, giving a settlement 'additional political and psychological force', he says.

(37) Interview data.

126

[38] United Nations document S/11818/Add.5 Annex, p. 9, 10 October 1975.

[39] Suggested by Yair Evron, 'The Role of Arms Control in the Middle East', *Adelphi Paper*, No. 138, IISS, London, Autumn 1977, p. 18. The anxiety that force levels within LFAs in the Sinai should not be exceeded has been a primary cause of tension between the parties.

[40] See Pelcovits, op. cit., p. 52.

[41] One view put by a senior British defence official is that the West Bank could be linked by corridor to a port, such as Ashkelon. In his view, the incorporation of the Gaza Strip into an independent state would produce insurmountable difficulties. As for demilitarisation of the West Bank and Gaza Strip, it is generally argued that it is easier to demilitarise part of a state, i.e. a Jordanian–Palestinian Federation, than the whole of an independent state. The Jordan River, says a former Jordanian Prime Minister, would become the 'military' but not the 'political' boundary and no tanks or troops would be allowed west of it. For example, in the past, when Jordan acquired American tanks, the delivery of these was conditional upon Jordan's undertaking an obligation not to deploy them on the West Bank (though Jordanian tanks did enter the West Bank in June 1967). The West Bank effectively became a buffer zone. See Dan Horowitz, 'Israel's Concept of Defensible Borders', Jerusalem Papers on Peace Problems, No. 16, 1975, p. 10. Moreover, King Hussein has shown determination in the past to stop border crossings. After the 1953 Qibya Resolution, he increased police and patrols in border areas, jailed known terrorists and organised weekly meetings between Israeli and Jordanian commanders.

[42] For the text of the PLO statement of the Palestinian position allegedly presented to President Carter in Summer 1977 by Crown Prince Fahd of Saudi Arabia, see *The Guardian* (London), 2 August 1977. This stipulates that an independent state 'must be able to arm itself with what it needs to defend its frontiers, independence and security'. Interview data.

[43] PLO leader Yassir Arafat's proposal (op. cit.) for a UN peace-keeping force to police the borders of an independent state is a recognition of this. In the opinion of the late Said Hammami, formerly PLO representative in London, a Palestinian army would not be the best guarantee of a sovereign Palestinian state. Interview data.

[44] On the question of Palestinian self-determination, moderate Arab states overtly support the Palestinian demand for an independent state – but with some circumspection. President Sadat is on record as saying that he is prepared to accept the Israeli plan for limited self-rule for Palestinians on the West Bank and Gaza Strip, provided it leads to eventual self-determination. On several occasions, he has indicated he would prefer that a Palestinian independent state should be linked with Jordan. See World Service New Bulletin, 13 January 1978.

[45] Because it may be impossible for all PLO factions to agree that a compromise solution of this kind should be final, a suggestion made by an Egyptian observer might be considered. This is that an annual plebiscite should be held for ten years in both Israel and the Palestinian entity on whether to re-unite former Palestine into a single state. Although this would mean that either Israel or the Palestinian entity would have a veto over such an outcome, the formula would at least leave open the possibility.

[46] Interview data.

[47] *The Guardian* (London), 2 August 1977.

[48] C. L. Sulzberger, 'US Hopes in the Mideast', *International Herald Tribune*, 5–6 November 1977. Also interview data.

[49] The suggestion of international trusteeship is not new. It was proposed by West Bank Palestinian notables when they met Secretary of State Cyrus Vance in August 1977. *Jerusalem Post International Edition*, 16 August 1977.

[50] Interview data.

[51] Interview data. Israeli governments have always maintained their inherent right of self-defence, including retaliation against armed attack. Nor have Security Council censures deflected them from this course. Israel regards the 1974 Israel–Syria Disengagement Agreement as a major test of peace-keeping. But since Syria refused to agree in writing to prohibit 'paramilitary' operations, Mrs. Meir extracted a statement from Washington in support of Israeli action in self-defence against terrorism. This bestowed approval on Israel's counter-measures. See Edward R. F. Sheehan, 'Step by Step in the Middle East', *Foreign Policy*, Spring 1976, p. 42. See also Comay, op. cit., p. 64. Statement delivered in the Knesset by Mrs. Meir, then Israeli Prime Minister, on the Separation of Forces Agreement with Syria, 30 May 1974:– The United States' position is this: 'Raids by armed groups or individuals across the demarcation line are contrary to the cease-fire. Israel, in the exercise of its right to self-defense, may act to prevent such actions by all available means. The United States will not consider such actions by Israel as violations of the cease-fire, and will support them politically'.

[52] By contrast with the Brookings recommendations for a gradual withdrawal which President Carter also favours, the approach outlined in these paragraphs is premised on a quick withdrawal of Israeli occupying forces – both administrative and military.

[53] However, Palestinians are said not to favour the idea of any Arab League participation. Interview data.

[54] This would go further than the present requirement that the UN peace-keeping force in Sinai should use force in self-defence including 'resistance to attempts by forceful means to prevent it from discharging its duties'. United Nations document S/11052/Rev. 1, Para. 4(d), 27 October 1973. It seems that the need for UN troops armed with medium or heavy weapons would not be welcomed by many potential *contributing* states, Jonah, op. cit., p. 117.

[55] Ibid., p. 115.

[56] India and Canada have been cited as possible states. The former Secretary General, Trygve Lie, had considered the possibility of a United Nations Guard Force which would have an internationally recruited permanent establishment with a reserve of national cadres on call. See *Public Papers of the Secretaries-General of the United Nations, Volume I*, selected and edited with a commentary by A. W. Cordier and W. Foote, Columbia University Press, 1969, pp. 166–177. Building on this suggestion, a Secretary General, staff officers and military coordinator could be responsible to the Control Commission, whilst men could be recruited individually as professionals. A force of this kind would have the advantage of military flexibility and discipline. Moreover, it would avoid national political repercussions arising from any particular incident. However, there would be the crucial drawback that the Soviet Union could not be expected to agree to its own citizens or those of any Eastern European state serving as individuals in the capacity of combat troops.

[57] Interview data. The British kept forces in Jordan supplied by air.

[58] Interview data. A lesson can be learnt from UN difficulties in this respect. See Jonah, op. cit., p. 122. General Siilasvuo stresses that difficulties in the setting up of UNEF II related to slow arrival of logistic units, poor equipment and communications. Lieutenant-General Ensio Siilasvuo, *Establishment of Peace-keeping Forces in the Field in the Light of Experience from UNEF II*, February 1977. Furthermore, the draft formulas for articles of agreed guide-lines submitted to the Special Committee on Peace-keeping Operations has drawn attention to the need for agreements providing that 'specific contingents' be available for a 'particular operation' and for member states to cooperate with the UN on preparedness arrangements, including appropriate training of selected personnel of potential contributors. United Nations document A/AC.121/L.27 and Appendix I, 4 November 1976.

[59] However, if Israel retained the right to conduct photo-reconnaissance over the West Bank and to retain remotely-controlled radar and surveillance devices on the western escarpment above the Jordan River, it could itself detect any attempt to introduce heavy weapons into the West Bank. But then the question arises: what would the Arabs want in return?

[60] *Financial Times* (London), 28 February 1977.

[61] *Financial Times* (London), 28 February 1977.

[62] *Jerusalem Post International Edition*, 23 November 1976.

[63] UN Security council Resolution 425, 1978. See also Report of the Secretary General on the Implementation of Resolution 425, United Nations document S/12611, 19 March 1978.

[64] See *Time Magazine*, 29 May 1978, p. 26. The Soviet Union also supports this view. *The Guardian* (London), 4 May 1978. But the UNIFIL Commander, General Erskine, has said that the Cairo Agreement is incompatible with UNIFIL's mission.

[65] The French contingent has armoured vehicles carrying 90mm cannons and the Irish contingent 20 APCs and a battery of 160mm heavy mortars.

[66] Key contributors have said they will leave if serious fighting erupts. *Newsweek*, 24 April 1978.

[67] John Barton, forthcoming Adelphi Paper on Guarantees and Sanctions for Arms Control, IISS, London, 1978.

[68] As suggested by the Chargé d'Affaires, a.i., of Greece to the United Nations, the UN should react 'more vigorously' to attacks. What is needed, he says, is 'a system of immediate, automatic and effective international condemnation'. Memorandum to the UN addressed to the Chairman of the Special Committee on Peace-keeping Operations and its Working Group, United Nations document A/AC.121/L.27, Appendix II, p. 8, 4 November 1976.

[69] In the same Declaration, the Four Powers would have committed themselves to a joint arrangement on arms supplies (see Chapter 6).

[70] For extreme cases, George C. McGhee has proposed 'air action based outside the area'. *The Washington Post*, 14 January 1974. Like McGhee, Sir Anthony Buzzard anticipated the need of air action based outside the area. He foresaw the failure of UNEF and of the Four Powers to agree in time, whether inside or outside the United Nations. Therefore, in conformity with Articles 51 and 52 of the UN Charter, he suggested the Middle Powers should offer a 'stand-by' guarantee in the form of air forces – 250 fighter-bombers to ensure neither Arabs nor Israelis would gain air superiority. See Parliamentary Group for World Government, Minutes of

Meeting held on 12 March 1970. The question of who would be prepared to pilot the fighter-bombers in combat missions is difficult. The suggestion lacks credibility.

[71] Interview data.

[72] These separate bottom-line guarantee treaties would resemble the 1960 London Treaty of Guarantee for Cyprus which empowers Greece and Turkey to intervene unilaterally – a device that worked until 1974.

6. PEACE AND THE NECESSITY FOR ARMS CONTROL

Stability in the Middle East will depend on the military balance of forces, as well as the political relationships, between the confrontation states. It follows that a political settlement seeking to stabilise the area must include arms control measures. These need not prevent Middle East states from maintaining forces and arsenals (though, as discussed earlier, a new Palestinian entity would be subject to special restrictions) to meet certain security needs, but they must seek to stabilise the military balance.

The difficulties of controlling arms levels even in the context of a peace settlement should not be under-estimated. It is true that, with a negotiated settlement, the confrontation states will want to shift resources to domestic tasks and that outside powers will have a vested interest in both underwriting the settlement and lending credibility to their roles as guarantors by exercising restraint in transferring arms. Nevertheless, there are at least three factors which complicate the task of regulating arms levels: i) inter-Arab disputes may flare up. Thus, individual Arab states will continue to demand arms, the supply of which would in turn upset the overall balance between the Arab states and Israel; ii) the chief arms suppliers are likely to engage in arms sales diplomacy from time to time despite voluntary agreements they might reach; iii) the sheer complexity of attempting to define a balance of arms levels. This having been said, what could be done?

Arms control measures could be mutually agreed by i) the chief suppliers to the region; ii) the local parties entering into voluntary agreements; iii) suppliers with the acquiescence of the local parties. In the first case, the chief suppliers would have to agree to stop transfers of destabilising (see pp. 141–143) weapons and limit the overall numbers of certain kinds of weapons. In the second case, encouraged by a peace settlement, with its accompanying safeguards and guarantees, the local parties might come to a voluntary agreement to limit arms imports and the deployment and use of certain arms. But political circumstances are always subject to change and such agreements might simply become out-dated.[1] In the third case, recipient states, in their own interest, might cooperate with suppliers in the regulation of arms transfers. Their incentive would be to divert resources to urgent social and economic needs, and to slow military competition in the region. But such acquiescence by recipient states could not be counted on: suppliers' attempts to restrain arms might be seen as discriminatory by recipients or they might be rejected by them as the result of a local political change.

Recipients' self-restraint might become a useful confidence-building measure and would certainly facilitate the suppliers' task. But in the final analysis, it is the arms suppliers themselves, who have fuelled the area with arms in the past, who must take the initiative in applying arms control measures. It is they who ultimately have the power both to reassure and to threaten. What is needed is their political will to control specific force levels and weapon inventories and bring the level of arms to a more stable balance. Stability may be achieved by lowering levels of some arms and maintaining levels of others. Indeed, peace in the area will probably depend in the end on the suppliers' ability to agree amongst themselves, and willingness to use the leverage they have to impose certain arms limitations. In this way, arms control measures implemented gradually after a Middle East peace settlement become not only the key to the military balance in the area, but also a means of persuading the parties to respect all parts of a settlement.

If the Super Powers and other chief suppliers fail to agree on arms control, a continuation of the present political stalemate and pattern of arms deliveries would have grave implications. Indeed, although both Super Powers decided that air-lifts should be avoided in time of crisis, the United States has massively re-supplied Israel since the October War. And Russia initially re-supplied Egypt and has re-equipped Syria.[2] In the volatile context of the Middle East, the volume and quality of the new arms race could trigger a pre-emptive war – more destructive than any previous wars.[3] Not only could a fifth war in the Middle East be catastrophic for the local parties, but it could again precipitate a Super Power military confrontation.

In 1973, Israel's Defence Minister, Moshe Dayan, ruled out a pre-emptive strike as ineffective against Egypt's air defence.[4] But after the war, it was understandable that Israel, which had always favoured a strategy of surprise attack, should enhance its pre-emptive capability.[5] Although Mr. Rabin, when Prime Minister, gave an assurance that Israel would not wage preventive war except under dire Arab provocation, President Sadat has made his own position clear: 'We are as capable as they of resorting to a preventive war if we deem it vital for our defense'.[6] This is a volatile state of affairs. As a former Pentagon official points out, 'Double capacity to wage preemptive war . . . is likely to lead to a highly unstable Middle East because the chief defence issue will be how to anticipate a preemptive strike from forces that cannot be stopped or recalled once launched . . .'. First-strike capabilities on both sides therefore become a hair-trigger for war: at the first indication of enemy attack, one must launch one's own attack, or risk paralysis.[7]

The combination of sophisticated weapons, pre-emptive strategies, worst-case analyses and the lack of crisis management machinery must produce a high level of military instability. There is also the fact of 'hostage cities': Cairo, Tel Aviv and Damascus are within range of air strikes. As long as cold rationality prevails, so will mutual deterrence. But rationality cannot be relied upon.

This dangerous stalemate might at some stage tempt Israel to opt for open deployment of its suspected nuclear deterrent. The Arabs could be expected eventually to follow suit. In an area such as the Middle East, the circumstances are quite unsuitable for stable nuclear deterrence. Military instability would have achieved its highest level of intensity.

The sheer destructiveness of any future Middle Eastern war must be soberly considered. With the deployment of increasingly sophisticated weapons, the risk is that the Super Powers would be involved more quickly in a crisis. They would feel obliged to throw their weight behind their *de facto* clients. Russia could still be expected to mobilise airborne divisions if cities such as Cairo, Damascus and Port Said were under threat. Washington would be likely to react similarly if Tel Aviv was threatened. The Super Powers might, indeed, feel obliged to intervene more promptly than in the past. A replay of the Super Power confrontation of October 1973 is perfectly imaginable, but this time with higher stakes.

133

Political Feasibility of Suppliers' Cooperation in Arms Control[8]

In Middle East capitals, it is frequently said that a peace settlement cannot of itself lead immediately to an atmosphere free of fear and uncertainty. While they do not pretend to believe that arms control can prevent war, both Israeli and Arab defence officials recognise that it would reduce the risk of war, limit the destructiveness of any future war and reduce military costs. They also agree that arms control would help build confidence. They, therefore, favour the inclusion of arms control on the agenda of peace negotiations. The Egyptians go further and insist that any arms control agreements be supervised by the Super Powers, Britain and France.[9] Valuable resources could then be diverted to urgent civilian tasks.

In 1975, four countries controlled 90% of the major weapons transfers to the developing world – the United States (36%), the Soviet Union (34%), Britain (10%) and France (10%).[10] In 1974, three-quarters of world sales of major weapons went to less developed countries, of which 56% went to the Middle East.[11] Israel, Jordan, Egypt and Syria are heavily dependent on the United States or the Soviet Union for major arms supplies, spares and replacements. Therefore, Four Power coordination over the control of the flow of arms would constitute a vital level and could be effectively used to enhance regional stability.

If they are fully committed to upholding a peace settlement (and without that commitment, any settlement must lack stability), the Super Powers, Britain and France must cooperate in arms limitation agreements. The determining factor must be whether the Four Powers (or at least the Super Powers) have the political will to render the Middle East more stable. Indications (including the joint American–Soviet statement[12] on the Middle East of October 1977) suggest it is possible, at least, that they do.

In the past, suppliers have derived some political advantage from supplying one or another confrontation state and have manipulated arms transfers as a policy instrument. But with a peace settlement, the confrontation states could be expected to reduce gradually their demands, allowing the suppliers to transfer less without political loss in terms of their relations with these states. Also, the confrontation states might lose some of their capacity to play off one supplier against the other.

All four major supplier states have had political and economic incentives for the transfer of arms to the Middle East in the past. France has always attached high priority to its independent defence capability. And, in order to maintain this, arms exports have been crucial in reducing unit costs in its defence industry. In 1975, approximately 30% of French-produced arms were exported. Although their small domestic markets made overseas arms sales more important for both France and Britain, the wider economic significance of such sales can be exaggerated. In 1975, French arms exports constituted only 3.5% of its total foreign trade, accounted for only 20% of trade with oil-producing countries, and supplied jobs for only 70,000 of the work force.[13]

With its highly centralised arms sales policy, France could restrain arms transfers without difficulty. Indeed, there are indications that the French Government might favour this with regard to the Middle East. Referring to a future French role in guarantees, President Giscard d'Estaing has stressed the importance of a reduction of arms sales or pledges by the major arms exporters not to sell sophisticated weapons in the Middle East.[14] French arms exports are in any case unlikely to maintain their present level because there are limits to the financial resources even of oil-rich buyer states and to their capacity to absorb sophisticated technology. This may well account for the fact that the focus of French interest is, at least partly, shifting from independent weapons production with a strong reliance on exports to weapons production in cooperation with other countries. There is also a growing concern about the dangers of selling sophisticated technology and destabilising short- and long-range weapons to unstable areas.[15] Nor should the international prestige that could be gained be disregarded: French participation in a Four Power agreement on voluntary restraint vis à vis the Middle East is likely to seem politically flattering to the French Government, provided it is matched by a market-sharing agreement concerning arms exports to countries outside the Middle East.

The economic importance of the British arms industry lies mainly in its contribution to the balance of payments. Also, arms exports, constituting 30% of British arms production, account for approximately 75,000 jobs and permit lower unit costs in arms production.[16] Despite the obvious economic advantages that the arms trade brings, it appears that, if a multi-national restraint proposal were forthcoming from America, the British Government would be receptive. Not only would Britain want to cooperate with an American initiative of this sort, but it appreciates that the future of the British defence industry lies in European cooperation. Any restraints that included other suppliers and that were seen in the context of future co-production and market-sharing would be given close consideration.

But without the participation of the Soviet Union, the second largest supplier of arms to the Middle East, control of arms deliveries could not be effective. Both a peace settlement and regional stability would be at stake. The Soviet Union's incentive to supply arms has been essentially political: both to support liberation movements and radical régimes, and to influence those countries near to its southern borders – an area of Super Power rivalry, where Moscow has sold weapons on generous terms on occasions in the past. (Moscow is increasingly demanding payment in hard currencies.) In brief, arms transfers have been considered a legitimate policy instrument for regional influence.

The Middle East is an area where the Super Powers share a concern to avoid confrontation, which in the past has led the Soviet Union to show tacit restraint. In its public statements concerning the Middle East, the Soviet Government calls for arms control in the context of a peace settlement. And one Soviet diplomat privately conceded that his government considered that arms control *must* be tackled during peace settlement negotiations.[17] Indeed, the Soviet Union responded favourably to Secretary of State Vance's suggestion in Autumn 1977 for talks on general conventional arms sales restraint.

The United States is the world's largest arms seller.[18] Not unexpectedly, therefore, opposition in America to President Carter's proposal to restrict arms sales comes from some on Capitol Hill as well as from the arms and aerospace industries.

Although both Super Powers have an interest in maintaining stability and avoiding entanglement in a future war, an initiative from the West rather than the Soviet Union seems more likely. So, ultimately, the responsibility for an initiative lies with America, the chief arms supplier, which must take every precaution to carry the Soviet Union with it. Dr. Kissinger has underscored that unilateral advantage and arms control are mutually exclusive: '. . . any attempt to achieve a unilateral advantage must doom arms-control' because 'the purpose of arms-control is to enhance the security of all parties'.[19] In May 1977, President Carter took the required initiative by saying at the London summit that arms sales would be an 'exceptional' instrument of American foreign policy. Moreover, he suggested to France, Britain and the Soviet Union that they cooperate in this field with the United States.

The arguments against arms transfer restraint are familiar: apart from the commercial advantages that representatives of arms industries emphasise, there are sensitive issues concerning the sovereignty of buyers and of discrimination implicit in arms controls, particularly against those states with no indigenous production. The most powerful factor of all is the reluctance of the suppliers to impose controls on themselves. But these arguments are counter-balanced by the dangerous international reper-cussions that the present rate of arms deliveries to the Middle East could bring about. There is the risk that arms in the hands of friendly régimes could one day be taken over by an unfriendly régime in this revolution-prone area. More seriously, there is the inevitable threat to regional stability and the consequent risk of Super Power confrontation.

If President Carter is therefore to give a lead to the Soviet Union (not to mention to America's European allies), an energetic initiative is required.[20] While there is no doubt that Moscow and Washington consider arms control measures as essential to a stable Middle East peace settlement,[21] the political will has to be mustered to take the necessary measures. What might these be?

Arms Control: Some Past Examples

In the past, arms control in the Middle East has been perfunctory. The Four Powers have engaged in unilateral restraint in arms sales to varying degrees: for instance, Britain has refused to sell to 'areas of direct conflict', and the United States has restricted the re-sale of weapons to third countries. France, too, regulates its sale of arms according to certain criteria, but the re-transfer of Mirage fighters from Libya to Egypt during the October War points to the need for coordination by suppliers over end-use clauses in arms contracts if these powers are to restrict effectively the flow of weapons to the confrontation states. Also, the transfer of licences and technological know-how and the sales of weapons produced jointly by suppliers all pose new problems for arms control.

Other examples of arms limitation have included the self-imposed decisions by major suppliers to withhold specific weapons systems. Sometimes these were intended to deny a client a specific capability;[22] at other times, one Super Power has withheld to encourage restraint by the other.[23] In early 1977, America, in the context of President Carter's arms sales policy, refused to sell the concussion bomb to Israel – an attempt to limit the spread of a new weapon altogether, rather than an attempt to pressurise Israel through the denial of arms.

One example of a partially successful agreement between arms suppliers was the formal Tripartite Declaration of May 1950. America, France and Britain guaranteed the integrity of Middle East states and pledged to maintain a military balance between Israel and the Arab states. Arms transfers were regulated through the Near East Arms Coordinating Committee (NEACC). The policy worked well for four years because the three powers agreed, without the opposition of a major supplier, on the need to impose a regional balance. When the policy failed, it did so because France supplied Israel with jet fighters in 1954 and the Soviet Union, excluded from the agreement, negotiated an important arms deal (Egyptian–Czech Agreement) with Egypt in 1955. Furthermore, after the nationalisation of the Suez Canal Company, Britain and France took sides with Israel to attack Egypt.

In the past, recipients of sophisticated weaponry have agreed to limit their use. During the October War, Israel and Egypt were both deterred from using their SSMs against each other's cities. This understanding was followed by a tacit agreement, negotiated via the International Committee of the Red Cross.[24] An example of a formal agreement on the limitation of arms deployment in certain areas by the local parties is contained in the Sinai and Golan Disengagement Agreements. There are also examples of unilateral self-restraint by local parties: Israel has undertaken not to be the first to introduce nuclear arms into the Middle East, and has offered to guarantee never to use nuclear warheads on the Pershing missile, should it ever acquire it. And the Saudis have undertaken not to base their new F-15s in the north of the country and made a commitment not to buy Mirages from France. Such restraint on the part of recipients is all to the good, but in the absence of a peace settlement and a suppliers' agreement, is of little import and carries little credibility. Since 1973, recipients have not only acquired advanced weaponry, but Israel has accelerated its own indigenous arms production capability, and Egypt has plans under way to do the same.

These examples show that the idea of arms control in the Middle East is not new, but that in the absence of a peace settlement, backed by the Super Powers, arms control measures have been ineffective.[25] However, they do provide pointers for more effective multi-national arms control measures in the future. In the context of a peace settlement that must be backed by the four chief arms suppliers if it is to be maintained, the possibility of a quadripartite agreement along the lines of the Tripartite Declaration must be fully explored.

The Form of Future Arms Control

A Middle East peace settlement requires that restrictions on the sale and transfer of arms and advanced technology should be jointly agreed and implemented by the four chief suppliers to the region.[26]

If such restrictions are to be effective, these powers would have to cooperate and agree on qualitative and quantitative restraints and their applicability to the various Middle East states. Decisions would need to be taken according to the suppliers' group's perceptions of each confrontation state's security needs. This means that restrictions should also be applied to states not immediately involved in the Arab–Israeli conflict. Thus, regulating arms levels would be highly complicated. Israeli arms levels should not be balanced against those of any single Arab state, but against the combined levels of its immediate Arab neighbours. But this could also mean Israel being stronger than any individual Arab state. And no Arab state would want to be dominated by a militarily-stronger neighbour, whether Israel or another Arab state. Egypt's requirements are partly determined by its neighbour, Libya; Syria's needs are partly determined by its adverse relationship with Iraq; and both these states' arms levels are affected by the military power of Iran, which has stimulated the purchase of sophisticated arms by the Gulf States. Stabilising the military relationships between the confrontation states will, in the longer term, require agreement on arms sales to the region as a whole. How far and in what form could the rival arms suppliers cooperate to this end?

Suppliers have employed unilateral self-restraint in the past, but have not always achieved the desired outcome. Differing perceptions of the military balance have led to misunderstandings regarding each other's intentions. Moreover, this form of tacit cooperation does not involve the regular exchange of views that effective regulation would require. Consequently, verification would be more difficult.

Another approach might be for the suppliers to agree formally to limit export of specific categories of weapons and to ban the export of others to specified states. The drawbacks here are obvious: for instance, the supplier states might have different ideas regarding transfers of weapons and related technology as these became yet more lethal and advanced. Similarly, supplier states might assess differently any political change in the area concerned. In brief, a formal agreement would lack the flexibility required, and would need to be so comprehensive that the very complexity of negotiations might prevent suppliers ever reaching agreement.

Another approach would be an arrangement along the lines of the London nuclear suppliers club. In this case, whilst suppliers have agreed to regulate exports of nuclear technology according to a set of rules and standards, they lack any enforcement capability. This drawback would have to be rectified if suppliers sought to limit the transfer of conventional arms.

If this somewhat informal approach were adopted, the regulation of exports of conventional arms and technological know-how could be achieved in the framework of a Permanent Standing Arms Control Committee (PSACC) of the four principal supplier states, with the Super Powers acting as Co-Chairmen. The Committee's full membership would have to be decided at the peace conference. But, as well as the main arms-supplying states, recipient states should also be represented. At the outset, those local states which had negotiated the peace settlement could be expected to participate. Eventually, membership should extend to Iran. Iraq, the Gulf States and Libya. The aim would be to persuade the recipients not to procure certain kinds of arms or only in agreed limited amounts.

Such a Committee could provide a forum for regular contact and exchange of views at the diplomatic level, as well as the flexibility that the difficult and highly-charged subject of voluntary arms restraint by rival suppliers would require. This would help the Four Powers to work out mutually-acceptable arms transfer policies. The Committee would also be responsible for the difficult task of verification and the imposition of sanctions.

The Committee would be expected to react to developments in non-participating regional states which affected Middle East security. Ideally, the Committee would operate in such a way as to show that it was in the interest of all Middle East states to participate. It would provide the diplomatic forum for the Super Powers, Britain and France to coordinate their policies and to cooperate voluntarily on arms trade vis à vis all Middle East states.

Arms Transfer Restrictions

To be effective, different sets of restrictions would need to apply to:

i) arms transfers to confrontation states from all suppliers external to the Middle East region;

ii) arms re-transfers from non-confrontation states to confrontation states;

iii) aspects of indigenous weapons production.

i) Those kinds of weapons that would destabilise the military balance between Israel and its immediate Arab neighbours would be considered for restriction of transfer: for instance, those that upset an existing balance, undermined disengagement arrangements, stimulated a local arms race, or provided incentive for surprise attack. Restraint should be both qualitative and quantitative. Ideally, regulation would include all nuclear-capable weapons. However, since systems already deployed are, in principle, capable of delivering nuclear bombs (Scuds, aircraft), quantitative ceilings should be set and there should be qualitative restrictions on new kinds of missiles not yet introduced. Secondly, although they already exist and fulfil a deterrent function, weapons capable of hitting cities should be restricted in number. Third, some new technologies should *not* be made available to these states.

141

It would be necessary also to consider limiting the overall numbers of certain other weapons delivered to Israel, the Arab confrontation states and to other Arab states in order to maintain a stable military balance at a lower level in the region. A slower rate of replacement would be one means of reducing the level.

Restraint in supplying arms by the four main suppliers to the region would require complex and continuing negotiations between them. A voluntary agreement will have to take geography and population into account in ensuring a fair military balance. There would need to be close examination of all proposed transfers on a case-by-case basis and decisions taken according to agreed criteria favouring arms of a defensive nature. The task would be to maintain a rough military balance between Israel and its neighbours despite their qualitatively different weapon inventories. The Palestinians, who would be dominated on all sides by militarily-superior neighbours, would have to be dependent on the protective system provided by extra-regional powers.

Any restriction involving a trade-off between Israel's technical skills and Arab numerical superiority in manpower would need to be adjusted to any improvement in Arab technical skills that the suppliers might perceive over the years.

At the political level, the present moderate régimes might be replaced by more radical leaderships. Again, a confrontation between Egypt and Libya or between Iraq and Syria would lead to a legitimate augmentation of weapons, if desired, in those states under Article 51 of the UN Charter, which recognises the right of every member to self-defence. With the advent of a more radical leadership, the military balance would not necessarily change. But, if in the event of an inter-Arab war, the flow of weapons to the countries concerned increased, thereby augmenting their inventories in the longer term, then Israel would justifiably demand a re-assessment of arms control agreements and a compensating increase in its arms levels.

Then, again, assuming an Israeli withdrawal to 1967 borders with minor adjustments, the geographical differences presented by the Egyptian and Syrian borders pose another difficult problem. Although tactical precision-guided munitions (PGMs) are most likely to benefit defence of territory rather than offensive action, the distance that a DMZ on the Golan could cover is limited. It is arguable therefore that Syrian static air defences (intended to defend Damascus) would enhance the possibility of a Syrian surprise attack from a strategically-advantageous position atop the Golan. Should Israel therefore be permitted some long-range PGMs for their deterrent value and as a counter-balance? Thus, the question of discriminatory qualitative restrictions has to be considered.[27]

In addition, arms transfer restrictions would have to take account of differences in indigenous production capacity. Therefore, restrictions should be carefully related to levels of armaments produced by all the recipients. This is not an insuperable difficulty. Furthermore, it would encourage the local parties to slow down the establishment of indigenous arms industries.

ii) The arms build-up in the oil-rich states along the Gulf and the possibility of the re-export of these arms to the confrontation states raises a host of complex questions about long-term stability in the Gulf and Middle East. The recipients, operating in a 'buyers' market, now have some of the most sophisticated conventional weapon systems at their disposal. So, Israel will increasingly include Saudi Arabia and Kuwait, as well as Libya and Iraq, in its calculations of the military balance in the area.[28] How can re-transfers of arms from non-confrontation to confrontation states be controlled?

Unsuccessful attempts in the past to restrict re-transfers indicate the necessity for more effective controls. For example, clauses limiting re-export of French Mirages did not constrain the Libyans from sending them to Egypt in 1973. In 1973, Under Secretary of State Sisco constantly admitted that there was no guarantee against weapon re-transfers from the Gulf States.[29] Regardless of legal restrictions, the suppliers have little power to control the way transferred weapons are used once they have sold them; nor, in practice, can there be any restriction over where the weapons are deployed, whatever the restrictions on re-export might be. Nevertheless, once it was evident that an unauthorised re-transfer or re-export had occurred, the PSACC could impose appropriate sanctions on the state that had violated an agreement on re-transfer of arms. The suppliers could either agree to withhold economic assistance from the violator, or, more seriously, to refuse to transfer further weapons permitted by the

143

Committee at the time to the offending state. Sanctions *per se* would be a form of leverage, and the threat of their use could deter recipient governments from re-transferring the weapons in question in the first place.

iii) Suppliers' tacit arms restraint in the past has encouraged recipients to develop their own indigenous arms industries. Israel, stressing the theme of self-reliance, now manufactures a broad spectrum of weapons from small arms to aircraft and missiles. Also, four Arab states – Egypt, Qatar, Saudi Arabia and the United Arab Emirates – have established the Arab Military Industrialisation Organisation (AMIO). But Israel and the Arabs still depend heavily on the Super Powers for sophisciated weapons and weapon components. And even if indigenous arms production should proceed unhampered, it could not meet the need for the replacements required in a war of attrition.

This does not mean that indigenous weapons production could not be a source of critical instability if one state made a big qualitative advance in production. Suppliers' control of arms transfers is likely to lead to greater emphasis on joint arms production and market-sharing between suppliers, particularly in Europe and between European countries and America. Therefore, restraints in supplying arms would need to be accompanied by agreement to limit the transfer of manufacturing licences, production facilities and technological know-how to Middle East states developing arms industries.

A Permanent Standing Arms Control Committee (PSACC)

The dilemma is whether rival suppliers can cooperate to the degree necessary on this highly-charged issue of arms control. Any voluntary suppliers' agreement for limiting arms transfers will depend on the checking and control of its implementation. Compliance with an agreement not to transfer destabilising weapons which have either not yet been supplied, or exist in only small quantities, will be more easily verifiable. These weapons would include those already discussed.[30] Verification would need to apply also to any agreed quantitative restrictions. Though less urgent than qualitative restrictions, they would be crucial in an asymmetrical arms race. The process of limiting arms transfers, credible verification and enforcement of any agreement on restraint through a range of sanctions would require an efficient supervisory machinery.

What form might this supervision take? It seems that only the two Super Powers possess the technical means of verification that are unobtrusive enough to be acceptable to the recipients. Enforcement could be most effectively performed by the four chief suppliers. If they are willing, those recipients which had negotiated a peace settlement and were party to arms control agreements could also cooperate actively. Representatives of supplier and recipient states on the Committee would have the task of information-gathering, hearing evidence, investigating and assessing the implications of the flow of arms to and forces in the area.[31] Voluntary exchange of information could be backed up with data drawn from all available sources: monitoring stations situated in DMZs, local and outside powers' aerial reconnaissance and satellite surveillance. The variety of sources would ensure impartiality. Gradually, the exchange of knowledge would produce what Leonard Beaton called 'cognisance', or knowledge of each other's situation which he argued would help foster stability.[32]

To support these verification proceedings, the Committee could have inspection points at which all arms imported to Israel or the Arab states would be physically scrutinised to verify that they were what the exporter and importer declared by type, quantity and quality. Although in purely practical terms, such an operation would be relatively easy, the political problems would be substantial. Nevertheless, the possibility should be investigated. An alternative and possibly more acceptable method would be a check on challenge procedure.

The security interests of all the Middle East states could be protected only if arms control measures were flexible enough to adjust to changed security situations brought about by a breach of agreed arms control measures. Should conflict occur between Syria and Iraq, Syria might acquire weapons from, say, France. These might more than off-set war losses and exceed the ceiling set by the Committee. Similarly, a further qualitative increase in Iran's military might could set off another chain reaction through the Gulf and confrontation states. Or unforeseen indigenous arms

145

production in any Middle East state could upset the military balance. How should the Committee react?

As well as its 'watch-dog' function, therefore, the Committee would have to provide a forum for expert discussion and consultation on the implications of changes in the military balance or of political change. To do this, diplomatic representatives of the Four Powers would need specialists at their elbows capable of assessing the security situation in the area, and the right to adjust arms restraint arrangements. Inevitably, proposed changes to meet security requirements as perceived by the suppliers would provoke opposition. In times of tension, the Committee would become a forum of debate with delegations explaining actions they may have taken.

If verification procedures are to be credible and effective, they must be backed by enforcement measures. These might take the form of sanctions against states violating agreements and/or guarantees to act in favour of a state under threat. Detection of a breach of an arms control measure (for example, a prohibited arms transfer) or of other developments upsetting the local balance, would need immediate referral to the Committee. The Committee would have ready a range of possible sanctions and guarantees, but these should not be imposed arbitrarily for fear of upsetting the complex network of arms control agreements; each act of enforcement would be an appropriate response to a given violation, and would have been agreed by the Committee during peace negotiations.

After confirmation that the violation had taken place, diplomacy and publicity would be used to persuade the violator to return to the *status quo ante*. Appropriate enforcement measures would be available for serious violations (the gravity of which could be defined by the kind and quantity of prohibited weapons introduced), whether an opportunistic act on the part of a Committee member, or the acquisition of prohibited weapons by local states from a non-member; the Committee could deny other vital weapon systems, components and spare parts permitted under arms transfer arrangements, or withhold economic aid. If this did not work, then the ultimate sanction of supplying off-setting weapons to the threatened party could be brought into play.[33]

To argue that Israeli indigenous defence production capability

146

(now said to supply 30% of Israel's weapons) would reduce the effect of the first type of sanction is to over-estimate Israel's independence. That very indigenous capability would be vulnerable to the withholding of licences, components and economic assistance.[34] Similarly, the argument that, in the case of the Arabs, the ability to re-transfer weapons from the oil-rich to confrontation states would reduce the effect of sanctions is a weak one. Re-transfers would not be automatically effective: for instance, in many cases, components and spare parts can not be inter-changed. However, aircraft, tanks and missiles and certain arms could be readily re-transferred (such as the F-5 operated by both confrontation and non-confrontation states). But, in the last analysis, Israeli and Arab states' dependence on the Super Powers – and to a lesser extent on Britain and France – would ensure effective sanctions, provided these were implemented in good faith.

The PSACC, but in effect the Four Powers, would decide on appropriate sanctions and guarantees.[35] With the Super Powers still the chief suppliers to the region, it would be their agreement to cooperate over arms control measures and enforcement action that would count. With their ultimate leverage over recipient states, it is the Super Powers who would render sanctions effective. If either Super Power surreptitiously supplied illegal arms to Middle East states, or refused to impose the necessary sanctions, there would be no means of coercing the offender other than by counter-supply. If diplomacy failed, the Middle East would return to its dangerous condition before the peace settlement.

The Recipients' Contribution

When discussing arms restraint, the suppliers on the PSACC would need to make judgements about the security needs of each recipient state. It is to be hoped that the suppliers' views and decisions would be acceptable to the representatives of the recipient states on the Committee. This would depend on whether suppliers' restraint conflicted with the self-interests of the recipients and on whether recipients believed that arms transfer restraint was being carried out in good faith.

The recipients would want limits on arms flows to be compatible with new strategies they adopted after a peace settlement; to be

147

sufficiently flexible to adapt to changes in the military balance; and to be accompanied by efficient verification and automatic sanctions. While the suppliers would seek maximum coordination with recipient states, arguments between suppliers and recipients inevitably would arise. Ultimately, the power to impose their will would lie with the Super Powers, together with Britain and France, all of whom after all are under no obligation to sell arms. As chief arms suppliers, it is they who have the leverage to keep the region stable.

The importing states might agree in various ways voluntarily to negotiate regional arms control. This would be for them to decide. Any understandings reached might serve the dual purpose of building confidence amongst the local parties and of facilitating the suppliers' regulation of arms flows.

Recipient states could agree not to import from any source arms over the quantitative and qualitative ceilings specified by the suppliers.[36] Traditionally, recipient states have opposed suppliers' restraint as an encroachment on their sovereign right to self-defence and have been unwilling to engage in self-restraint. However, it may be that the Middle East states would not automatically oppose suppliers' restrictions. After all, they have strong reasons to limit weapons procurement: resources are needed for social and economic development and local arms races increase political tension and the risks of incidents and war.[37]

It is not in doubt that some recipient states are capable of arms limitation agreements. The 1974 Syria–Israel Disengagement Agreement and the two agreements between Egypt and Israel demonstrated that those states could agree on limiting the deployment of forces and arms in specific battle-field areas. With a peace settlement which satisfied Arab demands for the return of their territory and for Palestinian self-determination and Israeli demands for peace, it might be possible to extend these arrangements to wider limitations on force structures, levels and strategies.[38]

In short, the possible interest of recipient states in suppliers' restraints and their own self-restraint should not be automatically excluded. Indeed, in practical terms, the recipients have a positive contribution to make. However, while this interest should be encouraged, it should not be taken to reflect anything more than what might be a transient gesture of good-will.

Summary

With Super Power cooperation and support for a suppliers' agreement on arms control, a peace settlement would be more likely to endure. Arms control would be the key to the security system on which the settlement would depend. This is because Super Power support for arms control would be linked by the peace settlement agreements to Super Power visible support (whatever form the presence might take) of international forces and safeguards in DMZs, and to Super Power guarantees of frontiers. In short, any local state threatening the international forces or any safeguard connected to them would be challenging its own material backer. The international guarantor forces on the Israeli–Lebanese border and on the West Bank and Gaza Strip would be designed to stop guerrilla warfare and reprisal raids; and other DMZs and safeguards would prevent minor infringements from escalating. They would also provide an early warning system in the event of a full-scale attack and deprive the Arabs and Israelis of opportunities to react to infringements with conventional arms. But it would be the Super Powers, as the chief arms suppliers, who would be simultaneously the major deterrent and the enforcement force.

The involvement of the Super Powers, and other secondary suppliers, in upholding arms control measures in this area would, therefore, be the best way of protecting the security interests of the confrontation states. The PSACC could provide the international framework for that involvement.[39]

The question is whether the Super Powers are sufficiently committed to a Middle East peace and regional stability to cooperate to the extent required. Evidence suggests that they do potentially have the political will. They have tacitly cooperated in the past to avoid being drawn into dangerous confrontation. Although without precedent, a Super Power role in maintaining Middle East stability along the lines sketched above would reduce military Super Power competition and the likelihood of East–West confrontation, while permitting political, economic and ideological rivalry between the Super Powers to continue. In short, it would represent a major step towards institutionalising détente at the regional level.

(1) John Barton, forthcoming Adelphi Paper on Guarantees and Sanctions for Arms Control, IISS, London, 1978.

(2) Press reports in early January 1978 referred to Soviet arms deliveries to Syria including SAM 6s and T62 tanks. The deliveries may have been a sign of Soviet diplomatic support for the Tripoli grouping in opposition to the Sadat peace initiative.

(3) See Amnon Sella, 'What Will the Next War be Like?', *Research Paper No. 13*, The Soviet and East European Research Centre, The Hebrew University of Jerusalem, June 1975; and Fuad Jabber, 'Not by War Alone: Curbing the Arab–Israeli Arms Race', *The Link*, Vol. 7, No. 5, November/December 1974, pp. 2–3.

(4) The possibility of international censure of an Israeli pre-emptive attack was another factor to be taken into account. But some Israeli military officials were less pessimistic about Israel's pre-emptive capability. See 'Israel Seeks Pre-emptive Strike Capability', *Aviation Week and Space Technology*, 27 October 1975, p. 19.

(5) In former Chief of Staff Mordechai Gur's words, 'The army is in a position today ... to bring about a situation where a pre-emptive strike will be viable'. *Jerusalem Post International Edition*, 18 January 1977.

(6) Cited in Robert J. Pranger and Dale R. Tahtinen, 'Nuclear Threat in the Middle East', *Foreign Affairs Studies*, No. 23, American Enterprise Institute for Public Policy Research, Washington DC, July 1975, p. 47, n. 17.

(7) Robert J. Pranger and Dale R. Tahtinen, 'Implications of the 1976 Arab–Israeli Military Status', *Foreign Affairs Studies*, No. 34, American Enterprise Institute for Public Policy Research, Washington DC, April 1976, p. 11.

(8) For an interesting discussion on the suppliers' perspective, see Andrew J. Pierre, 'Multinational Restraints on Arms Transfers', in Andrew J. Pierre (Ed.), *The Arms Trade and Foreign Policy*, (forthcoming), 1978; and Helga Haftendorn, 'The Proliferation of Conventional Arms', in 'The Diffusion of Power', *Adelphi Paper*, No. 133, IISS, London, Spring 1977.

(9) Interview data.

(10) *SIPRI Yearbook*, 1976, p. 253.

(11) Ibid.

(12) For text, see *The Times* (London), 3 October 1977.

(13) Pierre, op. cit.

(14) *International Herald Tribune*, 3 January 1978. In an interview, the French Foreign Minister has said: '... an agreement on restraint on the delivery of arms could be worked out with the agreement of the interested parties'. He maintained that this would defuse the situation and prevent new confrontation. Moreover, France would not be a big loser, he said. *The Middle East*, July 1977, pp. 34–35.

(15) *International Herald Tribune*, 27 July 1977.

(16) Pierre, op. cit.

(17) Interview data.

(18) In 1974 and 1975, American arms sales to the Gulf alone totalled nearly $4.5b., over half the total American exports. David Schoenbaum, 'Regional Arms Control and Proliferation: The Persian Gulf', (unpublished paper), 1976. For another figure, see G. Kemp, 'The Military Build-Up: Arms Control or Arms Trade?', *Adelphi Paper*, No. 114, IISS, London, Spring 1975, p. 31. Arms sales account for 10% of American exports and 400,000 jobs in 363 of 435 Congressional districts. *The Persian Gulf*, Hearings before the Special Subcommittee on

Investigations of the Committee on International Relations, House of Representatives, Washington, 1976, pp. 19–21.

[19] Henry Kissinger, *The Necessity for Choice*, New York, 1961, p. 284.

[20] This would be supported by Paul C. Warnke, the Director of the Arms Control and Disarmament Agency, the American Enterprise Institute for Public Policy Research in Washington, senior Pentagon officials, Secretary Vance and prominent Senators who prefer to remain un-named. In May 1978, at the UN Special Session on Disarmament, Vice-President Mondale unveiled an eight-point plan of action which the US would like to see adopted. This called for a strengthening and expanding of regional arms control arrangements. *The Times* (London), 25 May 1978.

[21] Interview data.

[22] America has been reluctant to supply Israel with the Pershing missile which it had agreed to consider for transfer in the Sinai accord. See 'Assurances from United States Government to Israel', cited in *Early Warning System in Sinai*, Hearings before the Committee on Foreign Relations, United States Senate, Washington, 1975, p. 253.

[23] Although the initial decision to supply F-4 Phantom jets to Israel was taken in late 1967, first deliveries did not take place till late 1969. Both this delay and America's decision to delay further supply of Phantoms in 1970 were intended to persuade the Soviets to limit their supplies to Egypt and to support the Rogers cease-fire plan. As it happened, between 1970 and 1972, the Soviet Union did refuse to supply Egypt with Scuds and TU-22 medium bombers armed with Kitchen stand-off missiles in 1972. And President Sadat suspected the Super Powers of collusion over limiting arms supplies.

[24] *Jerusalem Post Weekly*, 8 April 1975.

[25] Sometimes the arms withheld were delivered, though only after some years and then only in small quantities. In the absence of a peace settlement, Arab grievances and Israel's concern to maintain military superiority influenced their respective Super Power patrons to deliver some of the requested weapons. However, the tacit understanding between the Super Powers to exercise restraint over the delivery of certain weapons has not been totally abandoned.

[26] For an interesting discussion of possible ways to reduce the arms trade, see *The Sale and Transfer of Conventional Arms, Arms Systems and Related Technology*, a report prepared by a working party of the Council on Christian Approaches to Defence and Disarmament for the British Council of Churches, London, 5 June 1977.

[27] See Yair Evron, 'The Role of Arms Control in the Middle East', *Adelphi Paper*, No. 138, IISS, London, Autumn 1977, pp. 28–29, for a discussion of the problems relating to short-range PGMs.

[28] Israel has warned that it is developing a strike force capable of hitting potential enemies as far from Israel as Libya and Kuwait. See *Aviation Week and Space Technology*, 23 February 1976, p. 23. See also *Jerusalem Post International Edition*, 16 November 1976, for a warning from former Chief of Staff Mordechai Gur that Israel is aware of the threat posed by Saudi Arabia.

[29] *New Perspectives on the Persian Gulf*, Hearings before the Subcommittee on Near East and South Asia of the Committee on Foreign Affairs, House of Representatives, Washington, 1973. Later, in 1976, the Senate Foreign Relations Committee voted to stop the sale of Sidewinder and Maverick missiles to Saudi

Arabia because of their concern that these might be used against Israel in a future war. An urgent appeal from Secretary Kissinger reversed their action.

[30] Evron (op. cit., pp. 28–29) has discussed changes in the mix of weapons systems with emphasis on tactical PGMs. He concludes that this may in certain circumstances serve as an instrument of arms control, but that it raises difficult problems. On the Golan and West Bank, where DMZs are narrower and surprise attack more probable, the Israelis might require long-range PGMs for their deterrent capability. This would only be destabilising if the Arabs acquired the same.

[31] To enhance the knowledge of UN member states on global weapons developments, the CCADD Working Party (op. cit., p. 4) has suggested that it might be in the common interest of the major groupings at the UN to transfer to it the information-gathering and publicity activities of the International Institute for Strategic Studies and the Stockholm International Peace Research Institute.

[32] Leonard Beaton, *The Reform of Power*, London, 1972.

[33] This would be a form of the 'Negative Guarantee' proposed by Mr. Duncan Sandys in a letter to *The Times* (London), 27 October 1973: 'I would like to suggest that, in addition to any other forms of peace-keeping machinery ... the United States and Russia should be asked to give a 'Negative Guarantee' that, in the event of renewed hostilities, neither would give any assistance whatsoever to the side which had attacked first ...'.

[34] See Hirsh Goodman, 'The Arms Imbroglio', *Jerusalem Post International Edition*, 31 May 1977, for details on the extent of Israeli dependence on the US for economic and military aid ($2b. per year), for avionics, computer systems, modern aircraft, and outside technology and know-how.

[35] In their role as permanent members of the UN Security Council, the suppliers would be expected to support the PSACC on arms control measures: for instance, there could possibly be prior tacit agreement between the permanent members *not* to veto a Security Council resolution recommending specific action designed to stabilise arms balances in the Middle East. If a Chinese veto blocked this process, the appropriate action would have to be taken by the Four Powers regardless of Security Council approval.

[36] The Declaration of Ayacucho was a precedent for an arrangement of this sort. Its eight Latin American signatories agreed, *inter alia*, 'to create the conditions which might allow the effective limitation of arms and put an end to their acquisition for hostile, offensive purposes ...'. But the weakness of the approach has been illustrated by the fact that the major signatories have since purchased supersonic aircraft and advanced weaponry and have accelerated indigenous weapons production.

[37] In this respect, Mr. S. Rajaratnam, Minister for Foreign Affairs for Singapore, in a speech before the Thirty-First Session of the UN General Assembly in 1976, had some strong criticisms of arms transfers. In his speech, he implied that developing countries were buying doubtful security at high cost, and questioned the view that arms control interfered with the sovereignty of these countries.

[38] The advantages and problems inherent in two possible voluntary agreements – a No Counter-city Attack Treaty and a No-First-Use-of-Force Treaty – have been discussed by Evron, op. cit., p. 34.

[39] In an article in *The Observer* (London), 25 November 1973, Lord Harlech discussed the need for a world security system linked to the United Nations which

would ensure that fluctuations in the balance of power would be handled rationally and peacefully.

Appendix I

The Sinai Settlements: Rafiah Salient

Early in 1978, there were twenty-three Israeli civilian settlements in north-eastern Sinai and the Gaza Strip. For Israel, the principle of demilitarisation of the Sinai from the Western Passes to a future international frontier remains a crucial one. But, in addition, the official Israeli position is that for security reasons the Sinai settlements cannot be abandoned or left without an Israeli defence. Consequently, Israel's Peace Plan, as set out by Prime Minister Begin, includes the retention of settlements in a 25-mile-wide strip of Sinai (as well as those in the Gaza Strip): it makes specific reference to the continuous existence of settlements within a UN zone with an Israeli military contingent to defend the area. To support this position, Mr. Begin said in early 1978 that although Israel accepts Resolution 242, it does not accept the interpretation that this means Israeli withdrawal from all the territories occupied during the 1967 war.[1]

But the settlement policy is a source of friction with the United States, which considers the settlements to be contrary to international law and an 'obstacle to peace'.[2] Moreover, the Israeli Cabinet itself is divided. Senior members, amongst them Defence Minister Ezer Weizmann, agree with the Americans that Israel's reluctance to relinquish the settlements could block an accord. In any case, there is some doubt as to the strategic validity of maintaining the settlements. Why is this?

Those who demand control of the Rafiah area as a security belt compare the pre-1967 and post-1967 Israeli security positions in Sinai. Until 1967, the Rafiah Salient had dominated the chief invasion route from Egypt to Israel. It was used in 1948; and it was in the Rafiah area that the Egyptians made preparations to go to war when they mobilised in 1967. Second, they cite the terrorist problem. Between 1949 and 1967, the Egyptians had been in contact with the Arab population of Gaza and were, therefore, able to supply terrorists with arms and funds for their fedayeen activities across the armistice lines. After the Six Day War, with the Rafiah approaches (and the rest of Sinai) under Israel's control, these Israelis argue that their forces could for the first time absorb a first strike while mobilising for war. Therefore, the principal reason cited in favour of retaining the Sinai cluster of settlements is that they would serve as a psychological zone as important to Israel's defence as any conventional military barrier. They would serve both as a deterrent to a full-scale invasion and to an erosion of a peace settlement by a gradual violation of demilitarisation provisions. Egypt could not move missiles or forces into this sensitive Rafiah area without the sure knowledge that Israel would retaliate.

Just as important, they contend, is that Israeli settlements here would help combat the terrorist threat.[3] It would constitute a natural barrier that would impede Sinai bedouin from smuggling arms to terrorists based in Gaza which would, under the Israeli peace proposals, enjoy limited internal self-rule.

What, then, are the arguments of those who doubt the strategic rationale of retaining civilian settlements? In the event of an intended invasion, the Egyptians would have to cross a wide demilitarised buffer zone. The desert spaces would give the Israelis ample warning time. If the Egyptians were intent on attacking, a small number of civilians in the Rafiah area could not deter them. With any infringement of demilitarisation provisions, the Egyptians would first have to move missiles and forces across a wide DMZ patrolled by the United Nations before moving them into the Rafiah approaches. The IDF could be expected to react long before this became possible. And, as for the terrorist threat, Israeli civilians on Egyptian sovereign territory could not prevent Egyptians from intermingling with them and would have no right to stop any smugglers of arms. In any case, it would be just as easy for Arabs to pass small weapons to Gaza inhabitants whether Israeli civilians were present or not: this could be done over land or by sea. As the experience of the Lebanon has shown, hostile neighbours need to be separated by high walls.

Apart from its doubtful security value, a continued Israeli civilian presence as conceived by Mr. Begin would have practical difficulties. Israeli civilians would be subject to Israeli law and

Egyptians to Egyptian law. So there would be no way of resolving legal and other disputes between the two local parties. And since Mr. Begin's proposal would permit free movement into the area from both sides, Egyptians could be expected to move into the area. Not surprisingly, therefore, the settlers, who are among Mr. Begin's most loyal supporters, have been upset by this proposal to hand back all of Sinai to Egyptian sovereignty.

Paradoxically, while the settler movement invokes the security argument for retaining control over the Rafiah Salient, the Israeli military establishment is less anxious about retaining a civilian presence in the area. Their concern is with the retention of the Sinai air-fields. The argument is that the Sinai has permitted Israel to expand and disperse its air-force and to carry out the increased number of training missions now necessary. Consequently, in January 1978, at the military negotiations, General Weizmann demanded continued control over three air-fields: *Eitam*, in Rafiah, where half of the settlers have work connected with the air-fields; *Ofira* at Sharm-el-Shaikh which gives Israel the capability of controlling the Red Sea; and *Etzion*, south of Eilat (regarded by Israeli officials as the most important air-field because it gives Israel control over the Straits of Tiran and enables it to protect the vulnerable port of Eilat from Jordan, Egypt and Saudi Arabia). But the chief fear is surprise attack. Even if adequate warning meant that 'planes would not be caught on the ground, Israeli military officials fear that a concentrated air offensive against the runways would immobilise the air-force in the same way.

The implication of this assessment is that while there is a security case for retaining the air-fields, the Israeli civilian settlements would not constitute a security belt and have no military value. However, it seems that the views of the proponents of a continued settler presence might well be dictated principally either by a psychological need or by internal party politics. If this is the case, Israel has to decide whether the settlements issue should now impede the road to peace. Could the psychological reassurance required not be met by international security arrangements?

Certainly, the Egyptians consider that the presence of Israeli civilians on Egyptian territory after the signing of a peace agreement would be in violation of their sovereignty. They, like the international community, consider the settlements illegal and in contravention of the fourth Geneva Convention and several UN resolutions. But Egypt does not rule out the possibility that the Israeli argument might be a political ploy to gain leverage in the negotiations – to concentrate attention on the Sinai settlements in order to draw the spotlight away from those on the West Bank and Gaza Strip. Indeed, Foreign Minister Moshe Dayan's remarks support this view: he said on American television during a fund-raising tour in February 1978 that in Sinai 'everything is negotiable'.[4] In a similar vein, former Chief of Army Intelligence Aharon Yariv, like some other Israeli officials, does not regard the retention of the settlements as a *sine qua non* of a real peace treaty.[5]

Could the psychological reassurance, that Israelis believe the civilian settlements in Rafiah provide, be met by international security arrangements on completion of a Peace Treaty? If so, how? Chapter 5 has described the advantages and disadvantages of two plans designed to cope with the security dimension of a Palestinian 'homeland'. If the Israelis are unwilling to depend on a UN peace-keeping force in the sensitive area of Rafiah, would a Border Guard along the lines described in Chapter 5 be a viable alternative? This would have to be negotiated with the Egyptians who would be asked to cede a frontier zone in northern Sinai of five hundred metres width to the proposed Middle East Control Commission. The Border Guard would have access to a 500-metre zone in the Gaza Strip as a condition of the creation of a Palestinian entity on the West Bank and Gaza Strip.

[1] *International Herald Tribune*, 9 March 1978.
[2] *USIS, Backgrounder*, 14 February 1978.
[3] The Labour alignment-led Government originally conceived civilian settlements in the Rafiah area as a means of creating a permanent barrier – before and after peace – between the Sinai desert and the Gaza Strip. This barrier was designed to prevent hostile persons and weapons passing to and fro between the crowded Gaza Strip and Egyptian territory, *Jerusalem Post International Edition*, 21 February 1978.
[4] *The Guardian* (London), 13 February 1978.
[5] *Jerusalem Post International Edition*, 31 January 1978.

APPENDIX II
MAPS

The Mideast, 1977

The British Mandate for Palestine, 1922–48

The United Nations Partition Plan, 1947

The Mideast, 1949–67

The Mideast at the Close of the 1967 War

The Allon Plan

Disengagement Accords After the 1973 War

Israeli Settlements in the Gaza Strip and Sinai

Israeli Settlements on the Golan Heights

Israeli Settlements on the West Bank

Jerusalem's Holy Places in the Old City

The Mideast, 1977

TERRITORY OCCUPIED BY ISRAEL
SINCE JUNE 1967

APPROXIMATE AREA CONTAINING
ISRAELI ARAB VILLAGES OF THE
SO-CALLED "LITTLE TRIANGLE."

LEBANON

SYRIA

Golan Heights

• Maalot   • Safed

Lake Tiberias

• Acre

Galilee

⊐ Haifa

• Nazareth

ISRAEL

Umm el Fahm

• Jenin

Samaria

• Tulkarm
Taybeh   Kadum
Tira
• Qalqilya   Nablus (Shechem)

MEDITERRANEAN SEA

Jordan River

Damiya Bridge

Tel Aviv

WEST BANK

Amman

• Lod
• Ramle   • Ramallah

Ramat Eshkol   Allenby Bridge
Latrun   Jericho

• Ashdod   Jerusalem   JORDAN

• Bethlehem

• Gush Etzion

• Hebron
• Kiryat Arba

Dead Sea

• Gaza

Judea

Gaza Strip   • Samu

• El Arish

Negev

0   MILES   25

EGYPT

SINAI PENINSULA

The British Mandate for Palestine, 1922-48

MEDITERRANEAN SEA

LEBANON

SYRIA

Haifa

Tel Aviv
Jaffa

Jerusalem

Jordan River

Amman

Gaza

Dead Sea

Port Said

Suez Canal

Cairo

EGYPT

TRANS-
JORDAN

Suez

SINAI PENINSULA

Gulf of Suez

Gulf of Aqaba

MANDATE

SAUDI ARABIA

MILES

0   25   50

Red Sea

The United Nations Partition Plan, 1947

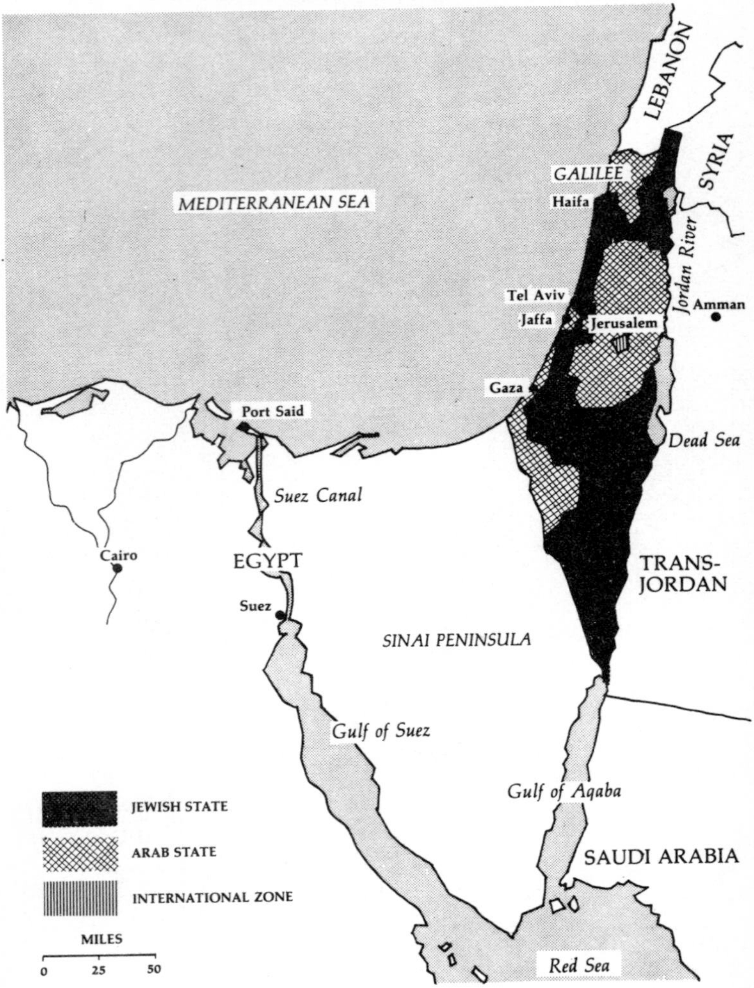

LEBANON
SYRIA
GALILEE
MEDITERRANEAN SEA
Haifa
Jordan River
Tel Aviv
Amman
Jaffa
Jerusalem
Gaza
Port Said
Dead Sea
Suez Canal
Cairo
EGYPT
TRANS-JORDAN
Suez
SINAI PENINSULA
Gulf of Suez
Gulf of Aqaba
JEWISH STATE
ARAB STATE
INTERNATIONAL ZONE
SAUDI ARABIA
MILES
0
25
50
Red Sea

The Mideast, 1949-67

© **Israelis Speak**, *edited by Larry L. Fabian and Ze'ev Schiff (New York: The Carnegie Endowment for International Peace, 1977). Reprinted by permission of the publisher.*

The Mideast at the Close of the 1967 War

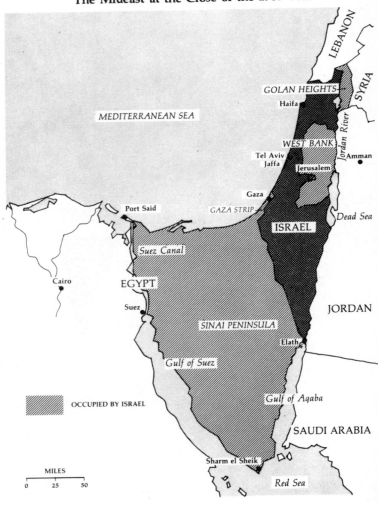

LEBANON

SYRIA

GOLAN HEIGHTS

Haifa

MEDITERRANEAN SEA

WEST BANK

Jordan River

Tel Aviv
Jaffa

Amman

Jerusalem

Gaza

GAZA STRIP

Dead Sea

ISRAEL

Port Said

Suez Canal

Cairo

EGYPT

JORDAN

Suez

SINAI PENINSULA

Elath

Gulf of Suez

Gulf of Aqaba

OCCUPIED BY ISRAEL

SAUDI ARABIA

MILES

0   25   50

Sharm el Sheik

Red Sea

164

The Allon Plan

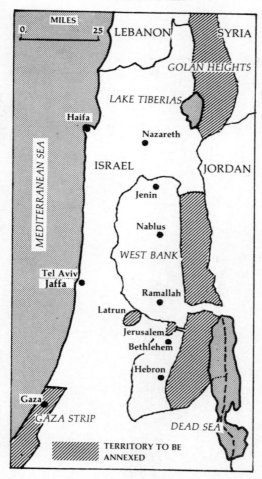

Map designations, key and shading adapted in simplified form from Ze'ev Schiff and Eitan Haber, *Israel Army and Defence: A Dictionary* (Tel Aviv: Zmora Bitan Modan, 1976), pp. 45-46.

165

Disengagement Accords After the 1973 War

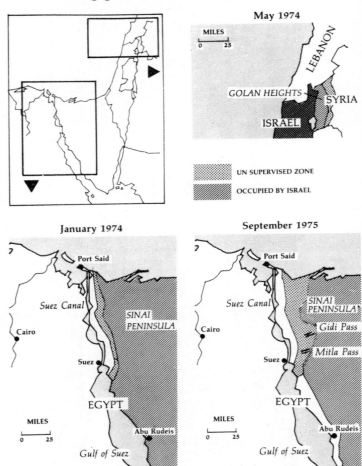

May 1974

MILES
0 — 25

GOLAN HEIGHTS

LEBANON

SYRIA

ISRAEL

UN SUPERVISED ZONE

OCCUPIED BY ISRAEL

January 1974

Port Said

Suez Canal

SINAI
PENINSULA

Cairo

Suez

EGYPT

MILES
0 — 25

Abu Rudeis

Gulf of Suez

September 1975

Port Said

Suez Canal

SINAI
PENINSULA

Gidi Pass

Cairo

Mitla Pass

Suez

EGYPT

MILES
0 — 25

Abu Rudeis

Gulf of Suez

Israeli Settlements in the Gaza Strip and Sinai

FEBRUARY 1978

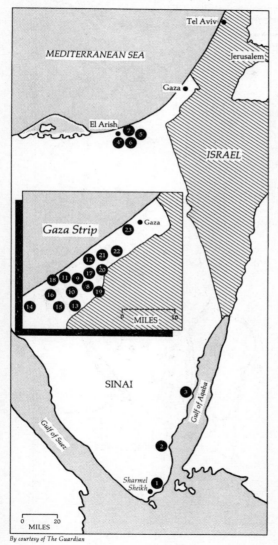

 ISRAELI SETTLEMENTS

——— ARMISTICE LINES (1949)

1 Ophira
2 Di Zahav
3 Neviot
4 Nahal Sinai
5 Haruvit
6 Nir Abrahaw
7 Tarsag
8 Erioti
9 Priel
10 Absalom
11 Suffa
12 Netzer Hazani
13 Netic Haassara
14 Dikla
15 Sadot
16 Holit
17 Nahal Succot
18 Yamit
19 Nahal Morag
20 Nahal Katif B
21 Nahal Katif
22 Fer Darom
23 Nahal Netzarim

By courtesy of The Guardian

Israeli Settlements on the Golan Heights

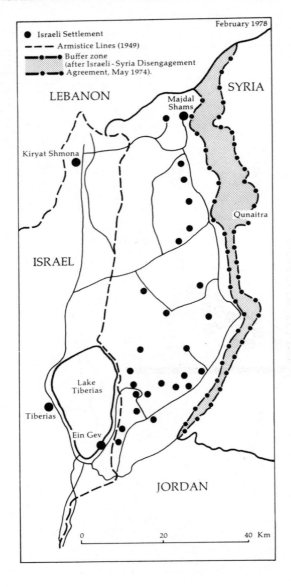

Israeli Settlements on the West Bank

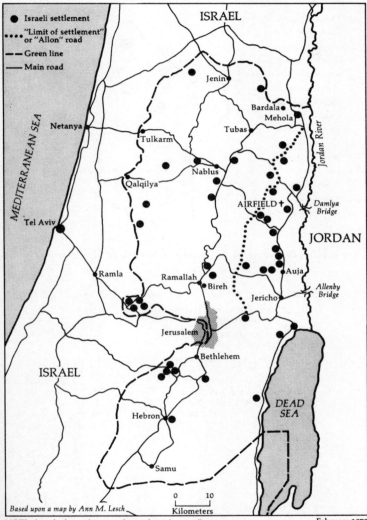

- ● Israeli settlement
- •••• "Limit of settlement" or "Allon" road
- – – – Green line
- —— Main road

ISRAEL

Jenin

Bardala
Mehola

Netanya

Tulkarm

Tubas

Nablus

Qalqilya

AIRFIELD ✝

Damlya Bridge

JORDAN

Tel Aviv

Ramla

Ramallah
Bireh

Auja

Jericho

Allenby Bridge

Jerusalem

Bethlehem

ISRAEL

DEAD SEA

Hebron

Samu

MEDITERRANEAN SEA

Jordan River

0   10
Kilometers

Based upon a map by Ann M. Lesch

February 1978

NOTE: Six suburban settlements and two industrial areas, all on the hills around Jerusalem, have been omitted from this map.

Jerusalem's Holy Places in the Old City

1. Church of the Holy Sepulcher
2. Church of St. Veronica
3. Mosque of Omar
4. Church of the Redeemer
5. Church of St. John the Baptist
6. The Citadel (Herod's Palace)
7. Christ Church
8. Church of St. Mark
9. Church of St. Anne
10. Solomon's Throne
11. Dome of the Rock
12. Wailing Wall
13. Islamic Museum
14. Aksa Mosque
15. Cathedral of St. James

Israeli Extension of Jerusalem Municipal Boundaries

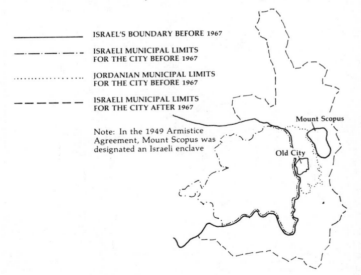

————————— ISRAEL'S BOUNDARY BEFORE 1967

—·——·——·—·— ISRAELI MUNICIPAL LIMITS FOR THE CITY BEFORE 1967

················· JORDANIAN MUNICIPAL LIMITS FOR THE CITY BEFORE 1967

— — — — — ISRAELI MUNICIPAL LIMITS FOR THE CITY AFTER 1967

Note: In the 1949 Armistice Agreement, Mount Scopus was designated an Israeli enclave

© **Israelis Speak**, *edited by Larry L. Fabian and
Ze'ev Schiff* (*New York: The Carnegie Endowment for
International Peace, 1977*). *Reprinted by permission
of the publisher.*

Abbreviations

AMIO	Arab Military Industrialisation Organisation
APC	armoured personnel carrier
CBM	confidence-building measure
CPSU	Communist Party of the Soviet Union
DMZ	demilitarised zone
IDF	Israeli Defence Forces
ITA	international transitional authority
LFA	limited-forces-and-armaments zone
MAC	Mixed Armistice Commission
NATO	North Atlantic Treaty Organisation
NEACC	Near East Arms Coordinating Committee
NOD	Night Observation Device
OPEC	Organisation of Petroleum Exporting Countries
PGMs	precision-guided munitions
PLO	Palestine Liberation Organisation
PFLP	Popular Front for the Liberation of Palestine
PSACC	Permanent Standing Arms Control Committee
RAF	Royal Air Force
SALT	Strategic Arms Limitation Talks
SAM	surface-to-air missile
SFM	Sinai Field Mission
SRSG	Special Representative of the Secretary General
SSM	surface-to-surface missile
UN	United Nations
UNDOF	UN Disengagement Observer Force
UNEF I	UN Emergency Force I
UNEF II	UN Emergency Force II
UNFICYP	UN Force in Cyprus
UNIFIL	UN Interim Force in Lebanon
UNMO	UN Military Observer
UNO	UN Organisation
UNTSO	UN Truce Supervision Organisation

INDEX

Air reconnaissance, 99
Akrotiri, 111, 119
Allon, Yigal, 22
Allon Plan, 23, 30, 37, 87, 100
Antarctica Treaty, 70
Aqaba, 55
Arab–Israel Wars, lesson of October War, 1
  1956, 2
  1947, 3
  June 1967 and October 1973, 20
Arab Military Industrialisation
  Organisation, 144
Arabs, Soviet role, 52
  joint superpower involvement, 72
Arafat, Yassir, 39, 51, 61, 83, 115
Arms Control, 17, 131–49
  indigenous production capacity, 143, 144
  recipient restraint, 132, 138, 147–48
  re-transfers, 143
  supplier restraint, 45, 51, 131, 134–37
  transfer restrictions, 141
Arms control proposals, 131–49
Assad, President Hafez al, 124
Aswan Formula, 124
Attrition, War of, 26
Ayacucho, Declaration of, 152

Bab al-Mandeb, 27
Begin, Menachem, 23, 39
Begin Plan, 20, 24, 27, 37, 82, 87, 100, 154
Ben Gurion, 6, 46, 60
Biological Weapons Control, 70
Border Guard, 11; and see International
  guarantor force
Brookings Institution Report, 42, 45, 52, 53,
  60, 71, 82
Brezhnev, President Leonid, 74, 76
Brzezinski, Zbigniew, 60

Cairo Agreement, 31, 116
Carter, President, 20, 45, 54
  views on settlement, 83, 92, 137
China, 52, 67, 110

possible veto in UN, 71
Clark, Senator, 50
Congo, 71

Dayan, Moshe, 21, 22, 41, 60, 100, 132, 157
Dayan Plan, 87
De Gaulle, President, 46
Demilitarised Zones (DMZs), 49, 83
  in possible peace settlement, 10, 31
  in Sinai, 89
  on Golan, 79
Disengagement Agreements, see Sinai
Dulles, Foster, 46, 53, 55

Early warning stations in possible peace
  settlement, 11, 49
Egypt, break with Moscow, 2
  peace demands, 82
  Resolution 242, 83
  US guarantee of Israel, 56
Eilat, 156
Eisenhower, President, 55
Eshkol, Levi, 21
Etzion, 156

Four Power Talks, 73–77
France, 45
  arms supplies, 135
  in UN force, 95
  participation in guarantees, 42, 71, 121
Fulbright, Senator, 47, 80

Geneva Conference, 68
Giddi and Mitla Passes, 97
Giscard d'Estaing, President, 135
Golan Heights, 28–29, 84, 90–92
  as DMZ, 93
Green Line, 87
Gromyko, Andrei, 75, 81

Hermon, Mount, 28
Hula Valley, 90
Hussein, King, and Palestinians, 31, 93

and joint Super Power involvement in settlement, 72

International Guarantor Force, 11, 13–14, 31, 87, 99, 106–13, 122, 157
   and UNIFIL, 118
   surveillance systems, 111–12
Israel, claims to West Bank and Gaza, 100
   defence treaty with US, 22, 53–58
   defensible frontiers, 5, 21–25
   guarantees, 23
   joint Super Powers involvement, 72
   labour government views on security, 29
   long-range strike capability, 151
   options on border question, 20
   Palestinian state, 102
   political dependence on US, 34
   Resolution 242, 83
   safeguards, 45, 98
   settlements policy, 24, 30
   Soviet participation in peace keeping, 67
   UN force, 107
   UNIFIL, 116
   Weapons production capacity, 146–47
   West Bank security, 87
   withdrawal, 19
   withdrawal from West Bank, 110

Jabal, Hilal, 97
Jarring, Ambassador, 21
Javits, Senator, 80
Jerusalem, 16, 86, 113
Jewish Lobby, see US
Johnson, President, 55
Jordan, US guarantee of Israel, 56
June War, see Arab–Israeli wars

Kennedy, President John F., 46
Khartoum, 1967
   Arab Summit, 21
Kissinger, Henry, 47, 48, 49, 62, 66, 80, 137

Lebanon, 16, 31–33, 113–20
   border with Israel, 84, 85
   Christian–Palestinian relations, 85
Likud, claims to Judea, Samaria and Gaza Strip, 19, 87
Litani River, 31, 115

MacArthur, General, 1
Maronites, 85, 114
Meir, Mrs Golda, 22, 41, 46
Middle East Control Commission, 14–17, 108–09, 119, 157
Middle East Peace Treaty, 71, 108, 110

NATO and guarantor force, 109
Near East Arms Co-ordinating Committee, 138
Night Observation Devices, 96
Nixon, President, 46, 72
Nuclear weapons, 21, 35–36, 133, 138
Nuclear Non Proliferation Treaty, 70

Palestinians—Army in Palestinian entity, 13
   claim to West Bank, 100
   demands, 101
   Palestinian entity on West Bank and Gaza
   military security, 142
      Strip, 12, 19, 123
   Palestinian security force, 106
   rights, 3
Palestine Liberation Organisation, 4
   Begin and Allon Plans, 5
   demilitarisation, 101
   in south Lebanon, 32
   Lebanon, 115
   Palestinian State, 37
   recognition of Israel, 64
   representation of Palestinian people, 20
   Soviet Union, 66
   UNIFIL, 115
   view of US intentions, 78
Partial Test Ban Treaty 1963, 70
Peace Now Movement, 38
Peled, General Matti, 23
Peres, Shimon, 48, 88
Permanent Standing Arms Control Committee, 11, 16, 140, 144–47, 149
Pershing missile, 138
Precision-guided missiles, 142

Rabat, 1974 Summit, 20
Rabin, Yitshak, 22, 133
Rafiah, 157
Rogers Plan, 36, 42, 46, 53, 72

Sadat, President Anwar, 24, 58, 79
Safeguards, 44, 92
SALT agreement 1972, 70, 78
Saunders, Harold, 42
Security Council, Resolution 242, 10, 19, 37, 83, 154
   Resolution 338, 10, 19, 68
   Resolution 340, 95
Sharm-el-Shaikh, 26–28, 88
Sinai, 25, 93, 96
   DMZs 84, 89
   political and security requirements, 88
Sinai I (Disengagement Agreement 1974), 48, 93, 99

173

Sinai II (Interim Agreement 1975), 48, 49, 68, 89, 98, 99
Sinai Field Mission, 50, 97
Sinai Settlements, 154
Sisco, Joseph, 50
Soviet Union, arms supplies, 52, 65, 132, 136
  financing of UNEF, 76
  Geneva conference, 53, 62, 65, 76
  and PLO, 62
  guarantees, 51, 52, 62, 74
  in UN force, 95
  Middle East policy, 64–67, 75
  Multilateral guarantees, 76
  Palestinian state, 66
  participation in peace keeping, 70
  presence in buffer zone, 49
  safeguards, 98
  step-by-step diplomacy, 52
Suez Canal, 26
  1956 War, see Arab–Israel Wars
Super Powers, arms limitations, 52
  cooperation, 8, 67, 77, 122
  joint guarantees, 63
  joint guarantees of Palestinian entity, 56
  joint policing, 69
  participation in peace keeping during 1973
  participation in safeguards, 72
      War, 10
Surface-to-air missiles, 90, 133
Surface-to-surface missiles, 2, 67, 68, 138
Surveillance, 96–99, 111–22
Syria, 12, 31, 83, 98, 148

Tiran, Straits of, 26–27, 55, 156
Tripartite Declaration, 51, 60, 138–39
Two Power Talks, 68

Ullman, Richard H., 47
United Kingdom, arms supply, 135–36
  and Palestinian entity, 39
  guarantees, 45, 71
  in UN force, 95, 121
United Nations

Charter Article, 51, 142
Disengagement Observer Force (UNDOF), 93, 95
Emergency Force I (UNEF I), 36
Emergency Force II (UNEF II), 73, 95, 109
Interim Force in Lebanon (UNIFIL), 32–33, 85, 95, 114–26
Manning of sensor lines in Golan, 91
Role in peace settlement, 11, 92–96
Truce Supervision Organisation (UNTSO), 73, 76
United States aid to Israel, 34
  arms sales, 42, 137
  commitment to Israel, 34
  defence pact with Korea and Japan, 57
  defence treaty with Israel, 11, 45, 53–58
  guarantee of Arab States, 56
  guarantees, 5, 45
  in UN force, 95
  Jewish Lobby, 6, 35, 37, 57
  Palestinian homeland, 103
  presence in buffer zone, 62
  security arrangements, 72
  Soviet involvement, 53
  Soviet joint declaration, 68
  stake in Arab world, 34–35
  view on settlement, 82–83

Vance, Cyrus, 136

Warsaw Pact, 29–31
West Bank, 86
West Bank-cum-Gaza entity, 5
  demilitarisation, 101–03
  political and security requirements, 100–01
  Security Council role in possible peace settlement, 11
Weizman, Ezer, 27, 156

Yariv, Aharon, 157
Yom-Kippur War—see Arab–Israel Wars